NOT-FOR-PARENTS

HOW TO BE A
WORLD EXPLORER

your all-terrain training manual

lonely planet

NOT-FOR-PARENTS

HOW TO BE A WORLD EXPLORER

Your all-terrain training manual

By Joel Levy   Illustrations by James Gulliver Hancock

CONTENTS

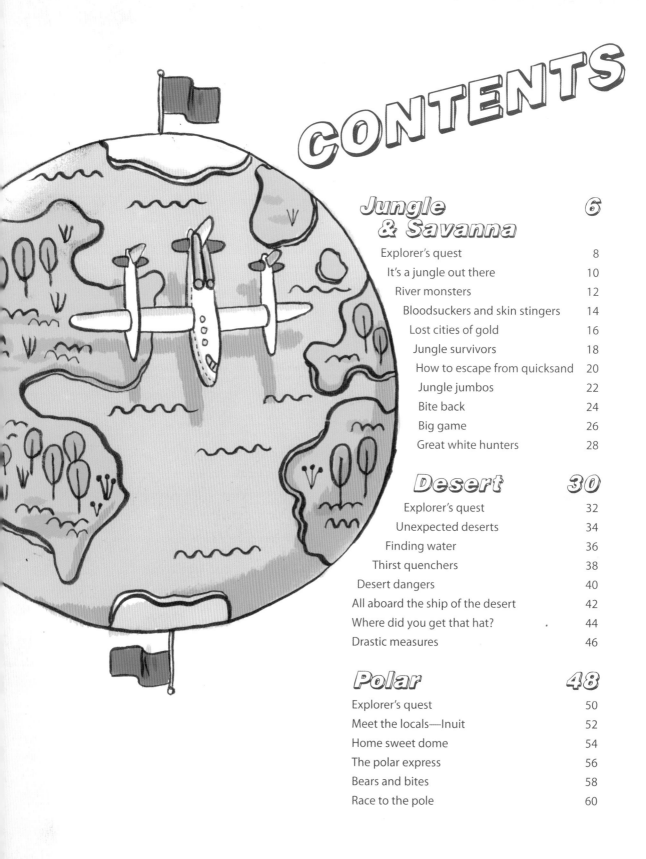

Jungle & Savanna — 6

Explorer's quest	8
It's a jungle out there	10
River monsters	12
Bloodsuckers and skin stingers	14
Lost cities of gold	16
Jungle survivors	18
How to escape from quicksand	20
Jungle jumbos	22
Bite back	24
Big game	26
Great white hunters	28

Desert — 30

Explorer's quest	32
Unexpected deserts	34
Finding water	36
Thirst quenchers	38
Desert dangers	40
All aboard the ship of the desert	42
Where did you get that hat?	44
Drastic measures	46

Polar — 48

Explorer's quest	50
Meet the locals—Inuit	52
Home sweet dome	54
The polar express	56
Bears and bites	58
Race to the pole	60

Forest & Mountain 62

Explorer's quest	64
Big bad beasts	66
Fruits of the forest	68
Meet the locals—Sherpas	70
Up, up, and away	72
Avalanche!	76
The Death Zone	78
How to rappel into a volcano	80
Explorers on Everest	82
Alive!	84

Oceans & Rivers 86

Explorer's quest	88
Vessels of discovery	90
Meet the locals—Polynesians	92
Ocean dangers	94
Lost at sea	96
Desert island survival	98
To boldly go...	100
Under the sea	102
River dangers	104
Types of river boats and rafts	106
Rolling on the river	108
Getting their feet wet	110

Air 112

Explorer's quest	114
To the skies	116
What goes up…	118
Afraid of heights	120
How to land a plane in an emergency	122
Cold air	124

Navigation 126

Map reading	128
True north	130
Compass 101	132
Stay the course	134
Navigating by the stars	136

Explorer Bootcamp 140

Explorer's essentials	142
The rule of threes	144
Fire starter	146
Camping out	148
Weather wise	150
Storm warning	152

Index	154
Acknowledgments	160

Can you find a lost jungle temple?

Mbuti pygmies—big in the jungle.

Watch out for piranhas! See page 13.

JUNGLE & SAVANNA

You're hacking your way through the jungle with your machete, when suddenly the ground gives way and you slide down a muddy ravine, tumbling through a giant spider's web and into a pool of deadly quicksand. The crumbling ruins of an ancient temple loom on either side. Should you call for your elephant, or grab a vine and haul yourself out?

Discover how to ride an elephant on page 22.

Can you fight a lion? See page 27.

Get jumping to the Masai rhythms!

EXPLORER'S QUEST

The tropical regions of the world, with their thick jungles and wide, grassy savannas, are rich in exotic animals and unsolved mysteries—in other words, they are perfect for explorers. Will you track down the lost treasure city of the Inca, or find the source of the Nile?

Lost city of the Inca

In the early 1500s, the Spanish conquistador Francisco Pizarro conquered the Inca empire, but some Inca escaped over the mountains into the Amazon rainforest, taking with them a vast fortune in gold. Adventurers and explorers have long believed that they founded a secret city in the jungle, which might yet contain a fabulous treasure beyond belief. Can you discover the lost city when so many others have died trying?

Welcome to the world

Thousands of tribes make the thick jungles of the world their home—some are so remote and isolated that they have never been contacted by the modern world. Can you be the first to introduce yourself to an uncontacted tribe?

APPARENTLY THEY'VE NEVER HEARD OF ONE DIRECTION

Finding the source

Victorian explorers were obsessed with tracing the course of the world's longest river—the Nile–and discovering its source deep in the African interior. Can you retrace their footsteps and make the exciting journey across the "Mountains of the Moon?"

Monster snakes

The biggest snakes in the world are found in the rainforests of South America, Africa, and Indonesia; some are over 33 feet (10m) long. But there have been rumors of much bigger snakes, so enormous that they could swallow whole canoes. Can these legendary snakes really exist, and can you stun the world of science by finding one?

Big game

For the big game hunters who visited Africa looking for animal heads to stick on their walls, nothing compared to the "Big Five"—the animals considered most dangerous and difficult to hunt: lion, elephant, leopard, rhino, and buffalo. Can you track them down and shoot them in a different way—with your camera?

Lion   Elephant   Leopard   Rhino   Buffalo

IT'S A JUNGLE OUT THERE

Jungle terrain is difficult to move through, and the combination of heat and constant rain makes it very uncomfortable—as do the swarms of insects.

Jungle anatomy

This illustration shows how the jungle is divided into vertical levels, with giant trees forming a thick canopy that blocks out most of the light. Down at ground level, the plants are crowded together, making it hard to move around; your machete is the most important tool you have!

How to use a machete

A machete is a long-bladed knife for slashing a path through leaves and vines. Get your technique right or you will waste precious energy, and take too long to get through the jungle. Always cut at an angle, and keep your wrist parallel to the cut. Chop down to cut through stems and vines, and up to cut through leaves. Follow a three-step cut:

1. Let your shoulder drop
2. Lead with your elbow
3. Flick your wrist at the last second

Emergent layer

Canopy layer

Understory layer

Immature layer

Herb layer

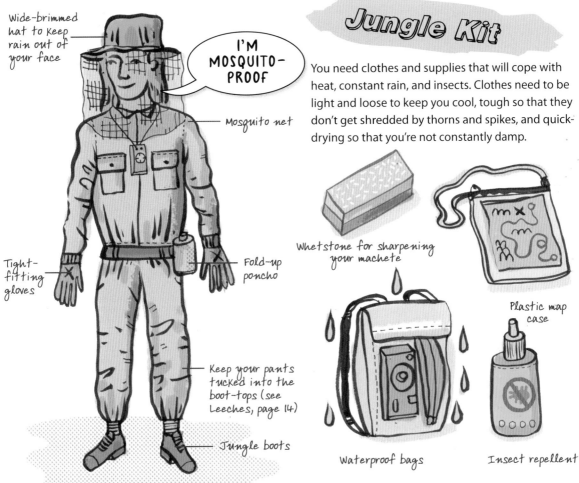

Wide-brimmed hat to keep rain out of your face

I'M MOSQUITO-PROOF

Mosquito net

Tight-fitting gloves

Fold-up poncho

Keep your pants tucked into the boot-tops (see Leeches, page 14)

Jungle boots

Jungle Kit

You need clothes and supplies that will cope with heat, constant rain, and insects. Clothes need to be light and loose to keep you cool, tough so that they don't get shredded by thorns and spikes, and quick-drying so that you're not constantly damp.

Whetstone for sharpening your machete

Plastic map case

Waterproof bags

Insect repellent

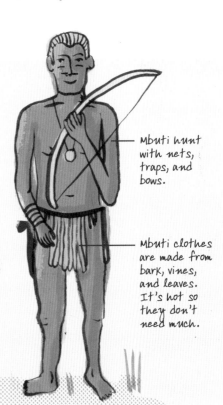

Mbuti hunt with nets, traps, and bows.

Mbuti clothes are made from bark, vines, and leaves. It's hot so they don't need much.

MEET THE LOCALS

MBUTI PYGMIES

The Mbuti live in the jungles of central Africa. They are pygmies, or short people. Although they do not write things down, they learn and remember everything there is to know about the plants and animals of their jungle home. They are expert at hunting. Some hunt with bows and arrows, others use nets. The Mbuti do not live in villages or towns; they build huts from plants, and leave them behind when they need to move on to a new part of the jungle. Their favorite food is honey, which they scarf down in large amounts whenever they find it.

RIVER MONSTERS

The best way to get around the jungle is to travel by river, but you won't be the only one in the water! Crocodiles and alligators infest the waterways of the tropical world—and they're not even the worst things.

How to wrestle a crocodile

Crocodiles and alligators were here before the dinosaurs. They are full of teeth, and horribly strong, but they do have weaknesses. If you're attacked by an alligator or a (smallish) crocodile you can fight back!

1 Distract or blind the croc. You need to get on the croc's back, but you could end up jumping in its mouth if it's not distracted—get someone else to wave and shout at it. If you're on your own, throw your t-shirt over its eyes.

2 Jump on its back. Aim for its neck, just forward of its front legs. When you land on it, push its head down—it can't do much while its head is on the ground.

3 Lift up its hind legs. Use your back legs to pin the croc's hind legs to its side, while keeping its feet off the ground. This will stop it from rolling over on you.

4 Blind the croc. Slide one hand down the middle of its head until you're covering the eyes; it will pull them back into its head. Press down.

5 Hold its mouth closed. Slide your other hand around its bottom jaw line, and clamp its mouth shut. Now bring your other hand down to hold the other side shut.

6 Pull its head back. Pull the head up and toward you. When the croc's head is pointing up, it is at your mercy.

Get a friend to tape the croc's mouth shut. No friend around? Oh dear...

Piranha safety

Rivers in the Amazon are infested with deadly piranhas—small fish with razor-sharp teeth. They attack in shoals of 20 or more, and can strip all the flesh off an animal in minutes, leaving just bones. Amazonian natives use their teeth to make weapons. Here's how to swim with piranhas and survive:

REMEMBER TO FLOSS BETWEEN MEALS

1 Swim at night—piranhas are active during the day.

2 Avoid low rivers and pools left behind during the dry season—piranhas only attack in shoals when they are hungry and desperate. In the wet season a river at its normal level should be safe, but in the dry season, when water and food levels are low, piranhas become more dangerous.

3 Chuck in some meat—throw an animal carcass into the river downstream, and cross while the piranhas are busy eating it.

River crossings

If you're trekking in the jungle, sooner or later you'll have to cross a river. The best way to get across is to fix a rope line and climb across, but someone has to go over first to set it up.

FLOAT AIDS

You can quickly make a flotation aid by tying the legs of your pants into knots at the ankles. Swing the pants through the air then thrust them into the water.

ROPE OR NAIL SOME LOGS TOGETHER

You can whip up a quick raft by tying a few short logs together with rope.

MAKE A RAFT

To cross a really big river, it might be worth taking a day or two to build a proper raft.

The only tools you'll need

BLOODSUCKERS AND SKIN STINGERS

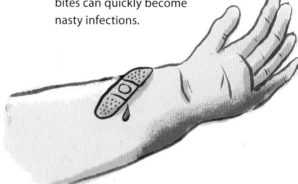

The jungle is full of adventure and mystery, but unfortunately it's also full of horrible things that want to bite, sting, and eat you.

Leeches

In the jungle, leeches are everywhere. They can smell you—stand still long enough and you'll see some dropping off leaves and squirming toward you. Leeches fix onto any exposed skin and suck your blood. You have to be careful about removing them because the bitemarks might get full of germs.

To remove a leech...

1 Look for the small end—this is its head. Use your fingernail to loosen it, then flick it away.

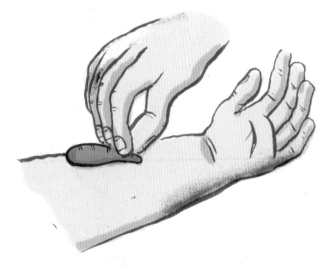

2 You can force a leech to let go with salt, alcohol, vinegar, or a flame, but this might make it vomit blood and germs into the bite wound. It's probably better to keep flicking or wait until it's full, when it will drop off.

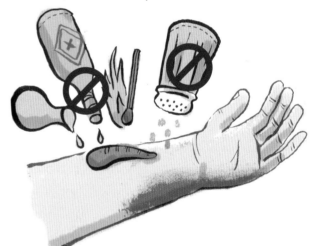

3 Immediately clean the wound with antiseptic—in the jungle even tiny bites can quickly become nasty infections.

Garlic won't help you against these little vampires, but salt and vinegar will.

Stinging trees

As if the animals weren't bad enough, in the jungle the trees are vicious too. Stinging trees are covered in tiny "hairs," like minute shards of glass, which are full of poison. They are so fine that they get into your skin, even through clothing, and can drive you mad with pain. If you can't avoid them, you can get them out using hair-removal wax or adhesive tape.

Creepy crawlies

The jungle is home to the greatest variety of insects anywhere on the planet. A lot of these insects see you as a meal, home, or target practice. This is especially bad news in the jungle because every bite, wound, or scratch is a horrible infection waiting to happen, so check yourself frequently and keep any bites clean and covered, and treat them with disinfectant.

BOTFLIES

Botfly babies bore into your skin, and wriggle about in your flesh. Learn how to remove them on page 19.

MMM, HUMANS— MY FAVORITE

BEES

In the jungle, bees are bigger and nastier than the ones you are used to. If you disturb a hive or swarm, try not to panic. Protect your eyes and mouth, and walk quickly away, through a bush if possible. If you have a clear path you might even outrun them. If you get stung, take out the bee stingers carefully with a knife edge or fingernail.

TICKS

These nasty little bloodsuckers clamp onto you. Some carry deadly diseases but don't try to rip them out in case their head parts break off in your skin. Choke them with tree sap or oil.

POISONOUS CATERPILLARS

Hairy, brightly colored caterpillars may be dangerous. If one lands on you brush it off with your machete blade, brushing in the direction of its head.

LOST CITIES OF GOLD

Explorers dream of filling in the great blank spaces on the map, and two of the biggest and blankest spaces in history were the great jungles of Africa and South America. Add the possibility of finding vast treasure, and it's easy to see why explorers were drawn to the rainforest.

DR. LIVINGSTONE, I PRESUME?

The two men had very different approaches to exploring. Livingstone traveled with a small group of followers and tried to learn about the people he met. Stanley however preferred to battle through the jungle as if going to war.

David Livingstone was a Scottish doctor and missionary. He crossed the Kalahari desert and explored central Africa, where he spread Christianity and fought the slave trade. Then he went missing on an expedition to find the source of the Nile, deep in the jungle. In 1871, the English–American journalist and adventurer, Henry Morton Stanley was sent to find him. After seven months, Stanley found Livingstone on the shores of Lake Tanganyika. The Scottish explorer was probably the only other white man for a thousand miles, but Stanley famously greeted him with the polite question, "Dr. Livingstone, I presume?" Livingstone later died while still hunting the source of the Nile, and Stanley went on to explore the Congo, the greatest jungle river in Africa.

El Dorado

Early European explorers in South America dreamed of discovering the legendary El Dorado (Spanish for "the Golden One"), a city of gold hidden in the Amazon jungle. Hundreds of men died trying to find this place, which probably never existed. The famous English explorer Sir Walter Raleigh tried to find El Dorado in what is now Guyana and Venezuela in 1617 but his trip was not a great success. His son was killed, his best friend shot himself when things went wrong, and his head was cut off when he got home.

Try not to catch gold fever. It has been the end of many a good explorer.

THE LOST CITY OF Z

Another man who believed in a mysterious city of gold in the Amazon was the British explorer Colonel Percy Fawcett; he called the lost city "Z," and believed it was a place of magical power. He had many adventures in the deep jungle, during which he claimed to have shot a 65-foot (20-m) long anaconda and discovered a two-nosed dog. In 1925, Fawcett disappeared while exploring the dangerous Matto Grosso region of the Amazon rainforest. Nearly 50 explorers have died while searching for some trace of Fawcett, but his body has never been discovered.

If you die in the jungle, don't expect a decent burial.

JUNGLE SURVIVORS

The jungle is dangerous and difficult, but it can also provide everything you need to stay alive—if you know how to find it. The stories of the *Gremlin Special* crash and Juliane Koepcke offer valuable survival tips for jungle explorers.

Cannibal crash landing

During World War Two, United States Air Force pilots discovered a hidden jungle valley in the center of New Guinea. The people who lived there had never made contact with the outside world. It was impossible for airplanes to land there, and the overland route was blocked by Japanese soldiers and native headhunters. This didn't stop military people from flying over the valley for thrill rides, and in 1945 an airplane called the *Gremlin Special* crashed into a mountainside. Twenty-one people died but three people survived. Thanks to the help of local tribespeople, they survived until a daring rescue was arranged, involving a glider and an airplane with a big hook.

Almost all explorers have relied in some way on help and advice from the locals—the people who live in the forest are the ones who know what to eat, where to get water, and how to stay safe.

The woman who fell out of a plane

Seventeen-year-old Juliane Koepcke was flying over the Amazon jungle in 1971 when her plane was hit by lightning and broke into pieces midair. Amazingly she survived falling from 2 miles (3km) up, crashing through the trees and landing with little more than a black eye. Everyone else on the plane, including her mother, was killed. Lost in the middle of thick jungle and with nothing to eat except a few pieces of candy, Koepcke remembered some advice from her father: find a stream and follow it downhill. Streams lead to rivers, and rivers will eventually lead to people. Following this advice, Koepcke walked for days along a stream until she found a lumberjack's cabin. By then, her skin was infested with baby botflies, so to get rid of them she poured gasoline over her wounds, and pulled out 50 larvae. Soon after, some lumberjacks turned up, and she was rescued.

Knowing some basic jungle survival tips can save your life.

Remove a botfly larva

1 The larva needs to breathe. Suffocate it with duct tape or petroleum jelly.

2 Apply pressure around the infestation point, and pinch the larva tail when it emerges.

3 Pull steadily until the larva is completely out. Clean and bandage the wound.

HOW TO ESCAPE FROM QUICKSAND

Quicksand is a mixture of fine sand, clay, and water. In the movies when someone steps in quicksand, they get sucked in, and the more they struggle, the more they sink, until they drown. Thankfully, in real life you won't sink deeper than your chest. But quicksand is very hard to get out of, and you could die if you are stuck for too long.

Sticky situations

Quicksand is strange stuff; it can change from being as solid as concrete to being oozy like oatmeal, depending on whether it is being stirred up. When you tread on it, you start mixing it up, so it gets oozy, and you start to sink into it. But it is impossible for a person to completely sink into quicksand because the human body is less dense than quicksand, so you will always end up floating in it —probably no deeper than your waist. Quicksand can kill you in other ways, though. Once you stop moving, the quicksand sets into its hard form, and it becomes incredibly hard to pull yourself out. This means you could easily get stuck until you starve, or until you're drowned in a flood.

Swimming in oatmeal

To get out of quicksand you first need to stop yourself from sinking in too deep.

1 As soon as you realize you are in trouble, take off your backpack, and throw it to one side.

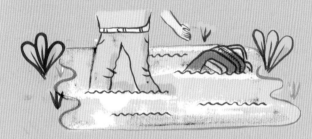

2 Lie down on your back to spread your weight. You should now stop sinking.

3 To get the quicksand to let go, you need to wriggle the stuck parts until they are free.

4 Once you are unstuck you need to get back to solid ground. If you have a friend, get them to pull you out—but make them do it very slowly at first or they'll pull your arms out of their sockets!

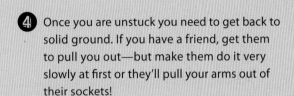

5 If you are alone, use swimming or snakelike motions. It may take hours to move a few feet, but you can take a break at any time.

BOOGIE YOUR WAY FREE

If you have a stick or pole, position it under your back or hips—it will help to spread your weight.

JUNGLE JUMBOS

Elephants are found in jungles and savanna grasslands of Africa and Asia. They can be fierce and dangerous, but their intelligence and great strength also means they can be a great help to an explorer.

How to ride an elephant

You can only ride a tame elephant (try riding a wild one and you will end up dead), and only Indian elephants can be tamed, so if you're in Africa, forget about it.

1 Get on board. Give the elephant the command for "lift"—it should raise its foot to form a natural ladder. Grab hold of an ear and put your foot on the leg, then grab a rope or part of the saddle and pull yourself on.

2 Practise giving the commands for "forward," "left," "right," etc. Use your knees to give nudges behind the ears.

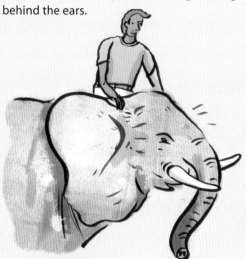

3 Tap the elephant's back. This is the signal for the elephant to sit down so you can get off.

If elephant dung is very fresh and wet, you can squeeze the water out of it and drink it—but you might want to hold your nose!

Survive an elephant attack

Elephants won't normally attack, but young male elephants sometimes become very aggressive, and females will attack if they think their babies are in danger. An elephant can gore you with its tusks, slam or throw you with its trunk, and trample or roll on you. Here's how to improve your chances of survival:

- Keep downwind of elephants and give them lots of space to start with.

- If one starts charging, stand still—running may encourage it.

- If the elephant has its ears out, it's probably a mock charge; wait until it's stopped, and then move slowly away.

- If the elephant's ears are flat, it's probably not kidding; find a large tree and climb it as quickly as possible.

- If there are no trees, throw a decoy, like a hat or rucksack; the elephant may start attacking it, giving you time to escape.

- If all else fails, squeeze into a hiding place or curl up into as small a ball as possible.

Ears out—mock attack, stand your ground!

Ears back—uh-oh, this elephant is really angry!

TUSK RIDER

When explorer Mike Fay was charged by an elephant in Gabon in 2002, he grabbed hold of its tusks and rode them, so that the elephant couldn't stab him.

CAN'T WE TALK ABOUT THIS?

BITE BACK

Most snakes are shy and want to avoid you, but some can be aggressive and may attack without much warning.

Mind your step

Snakes can feel vibrations, so one of the best ways to avoid getting bitten is to stomp. But watch where you're stomping! When walking in the jungle or savanna, look at the ground to make sure you're not treading on a snake. When you come to a log, don't step over it without looking on the other side.

What to do if you are bitten

Don't panic! Most snakes are not venomous, and even venomous ones don't always inject you with venom when they bite.

- Remember what bit you—you need to describe the snake so you can get the right antivenom.

- Apply a wide pressure bandage over the entire limb.

- Lower your arm/leg—keep the bite below the rest of your body to slow the spread of venom.

- Stay still—if you're with someone, send them to get help, while you stay as still as possible. This will help keep your circulation slow and slow down the spread of venom.

- Drink lots of water.

What snake is that?

Send for help

Drink water

Snakes to avoid

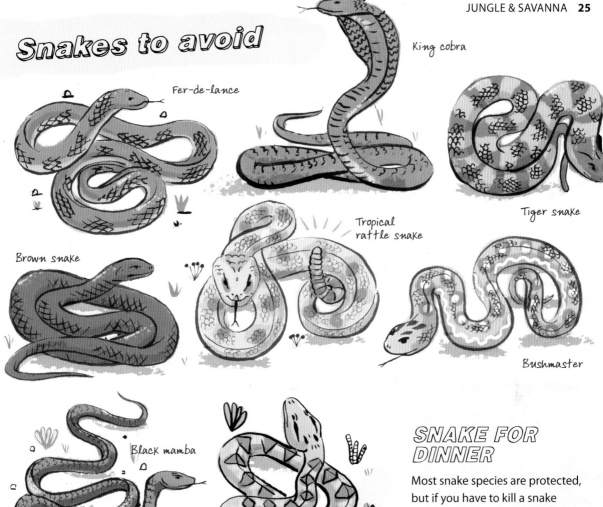

King cobra

Fer-de-lance

Tiger snake

Brown snake

Tropical rattle snake

Bushmaster

Black mamba

Coastal taipan

SNAKE FOR DINNER

Most snake species are protected, but if you have to kill a snake because you are starving, your best bet is to break its back with a heavy stick or club. Aim for just below its head. Use a forked stick to hold its head still, and then cut off the head with your machete, but be careful—dead snakes can still bite you!

MEET THE LOCALS

MASAI

The Masai or Maasai live in Africa's Rift Valley in Kenya and Tanzania. They love their special hump-backed zebu cows because they give the Masai everything they need—especially milk and blood to drink. Young Masai men, called Moran, go out and live on the savanna to learn how to hunt and fight. The bravest Moran hunt lions using only a club.

Jumping is the most important move to master when dancing Masai style.

BIG GAME

The African savanna is famous for its big beasts, but the ones you have to watch out for aren't the obvious ones, like the lion and the leopard—although these can be dangerous. So what is the animal that's polished off the most explorers? Believe it or not, it's the hippo.

Horrible hippos

Hippos are bad-tempered, unpredictable, and have huge chomping teeth. They can run faster than you, and climb steep river banks, but they are most dangerous in the water. As an explorer, you depend on rivers and lakes to get around, but as far as the hippo is concerned, this just makes you a target. Hippos like to come up underneath boats, overturn them, and then chomp people. Another charming habit of the hippo is to spray poop out of its rear end, while twirling its tail like a propeller, and spraying muck in all directions.

Buffalo bash

As an explorer, you are more interested in shooting animals with a camera than a gun, but the Cape buffalo doesn't know that. This animal is the ultimate enemy for the big game hunter—if you shoot one, it just gets angrier. Cape buffalo can weigh up to 2,200 pounds (1 tonne), and can run at 35mph (55km/h). In Africa, they are nicknamed the "Black Death'" because they are so mean.

Hungry birds provide a buffalo bug cleaning service.

Lethal lions

Lions generally don't attack humans, although sometimes they go bad and become terrifying man-eaters (see page 28–29). If a lion is coming for you, and you are stuck in the open, do not run! Stand your ground and wave your arms to make yourself look bigger. Hopefully the lion is only mock charging you, but if it is for real you have two options. You can play dead by lying down on your front, and hope the lion loses interest. Or if the lion is definitely trying to eat you, thrash and yell—it might put the lion off.

Leaping leopards

The leopard's spots help it to move stealthily through the shadows.

Leopards are the least likely of all these animals to attack you—they generally avoid humans. Only if they are wounded or ill are they likely to become dangerous. Keep safe by staying away from leopard cubs, and if a leopard charges you, shout, clap your hands, and wave your arms to deter it.

GREAT WHITE HUNTERS

The Nile is the longest river in the world, and for thousands of years it was the most mysterious. What strange lands does it flow through? Where does it start? The hunt for the source of the Nile was one of the great prizes in the history of exploration.

Mediterranean Sea

Lake Victoria

THE LAKE DISTRICT

In 1857, the English explorers Richard Burton and John Hanning Speke set off from the East African coast toward a series of lakes they had heard rumors about. After struggling for months with terrible illness and unfriendly locals, they reached Lake Tanganyika in 1858. Burton was too ill to go much further, but Speke went north and discovered Lake Victoria, which he believed to be the source of the Nile.

The two men argued about whether it really was the source of the Nile, so Speke returned there in 1862, trying to prove it once and for all. Although he found the place where the Nile flows out of Lake Victoria, he was not able to follow the river all the way down because of hostile natives. In 1864, a day before the two men were supposed to meet in public to discuss their argument, Speke shot himself while out hunting. Was it an accident, or was he so upset about falling out with his former friend that he did it on purpose?

Man-Eaters of Tsavo

There are few lands to explore that are empty of people. Make sure you can communicate with the locals, and remember that you are a guest—be polite at all times!

Burton and Speke didn't go exploring alone. This is what they took with them:

* 36 African porters
* 30 pack donkeys (with 4 donkey drivers)
* 13 Pakistani soldiers
* 10 slaves to carry the soldier's guns
* 1 ironclad boat

Colonel John Henry Patterson was a surveyor who was in charge of a British scheme to build a railroad bridge across the Tsavo River in East Africa. The project was stopped in March 1898, when man-eating lions started attacking and killing the railroad workers. According to Patterson, two large male lions killed 135 people. Their spooky ability to get through fences and sneak past guards led the terrified workers to call them the "Ghost" and the "Darkness."

Patterson spent months trying to shoot the lions, finally managing to kill the first one in December and the second one a few weeks later. The first lion was almost 10 feet (3m) long, and it took eight men to carry the body. It turned out that at least one of the lions had dental problems, which meant it could not hunt its normal meals, and turned to hunting humans instead.

Big cats usually only turn into man-eaters when they are too sick to hunt their normal food—humans are easier to catch!

Camels are well suited to desert life and make the perfect explorer's companion. Learn how to tame one on page 43.

Careful with that cactus! It could be poisonous (see page 38).

The Australian thorny devil—a very prickly character.

The shovel-snouted lizard dances on hot desert sands to keep its feet cool.

A jerboa—cute unless you're a beetle.

WHERE'S THE ICE CREAM TRUCK?

DESERT

An enormous sand dune as high as a three-story building blocks your way. Soon it will be hot enough to fry an egg on your water bottle, and the sand will start to burn your feet through your boots. Can you uncover the hidden mysteries of the desert, armed with little more than a bad-tempered camel, a plastic bag, and a headscarf soaked with pee?

Learn about the Tuareg on page 39.

Tok Tokkie beetles have a clever way of collecting water—with their butts!

EXPLORER'S QUEST

The desert conceals incredible secrets and undiscovered mysteries, from lost armies of the ancient world to the most extreme animals on Earth. What will you discover?

The lost army of Cambyses

Cambyses was a Persian emperor and conqueror of Egypt. In the year 252 BC he sent a massive army of 50,000 heavily armed warriors to invade the mysterious oasis kingdom of Siwa, where the great temple of the Egyptian god Amun-Ra was located. A huge sandstorm swallowed up the army as they struggled across the desert, and they vanished without a trace—every single one of them. The last resting place of Cambyses' army remains one of history's great mysteries. Located deep within Egypt's forbidding Western Desert, where boiling winds of over 100°F (40°C) blow for days on end, this warrior's graveyard would be a priceless treasure trove of ancient weapons and other relics, winning fortune and glory for the explorer who discovers its whereabouts.

ROCK ART OF THE DEEP DESERT

On a rocky plateau hidden deep within the Sahara is remarkable evidence that the world's most enormous desert was once a lush watery paradise. Prehistoric rock art shows animals that lived here over 6,500 years ago, including giraffes, crocodiles, and hippos. Once there must have been rivers and lakes here, but now there is only sand and rock. Can you track down these ancient and sacred artworks?

Extreme animals of the desert

In the hellish desert environment it seems impossible that anything could survive, but there are animals who can take the heat. These special species have unique adaptations that allow them to resist the heat and survive with little water. Can you discover which animal is the ultimate desert survivor?

Camels can lose up to 40 percent of the water from their blood and still survive.

Kangaroo rats of North America's hottest deserts such as the Mojave and Sonoran, build air-conditioned burrows and never need to drink.

Tok tokkie or fog basking beetles stick their butts in the air during the frosty desert mornings, so that dew will collect on their behinds, and run down to their mouths.

I NEVER TOUCH A DROP, THANKS

Kangaroo rat

Tok tokkie beetle

UNEXPECTED DESERTS

The popular image of a desert is of sand dunes as far as the eye can see, but there is more to deserts than just sand. The deserts of the world include an amazing variety of landscapes and even temperatures—remember, what makes a desert isn't heat, but lack of water.

Driest desert

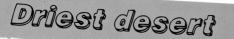

Rain shadow here

Mountain range

The driest place on Earth is the Atacama Desert in South America. There are parts of this desert where it has never rained—at least not since records began. Why is it so dry? The tall mountains that separate the Atacama from the jungles of the Amazon Basin form an impassable barrier for rain clouds. All the rain falls on the mountains, leaving the Atacama desert in their "rain shadow."

Skyscraper sand dunes

Sand dunes form where the wind piles up sand. If you've only ever seen a dune at the beach, it can be a shock to realize that tiny grains of loose sand can pile up into giant mountains over almost 1,000 feet (300m) high—as tall as a skyscraper.

The Empty Quarter

The immense desert known in Arabic as the Rub al Khali ("the quarter of emptiness") is what you think of when you close your eyes and imagine a desert—a vast, endless stretch of sand known as a sand sea. In fact it is the largest sand sea on Earth. Crossing this sandy wasteland is seen as the ultimate challenge for the desert explorer.

Cold deserts

Deserts like the Gobi Desert of central Asia get extremely cold because they are high up. In the Gobi it is common to see frost on sand dunes. The coldest desert in the world is actually made of water—in the form of ice! In the middle of Antarctica it never rains and hardly ever snows.

MY COUSIN ERNIE IS A CAMEL

FINDING WATER

You can lose up to a quarter of a gallon of water an hour in the desert. Since deserts by definition are very dry places, you're not likely to find this much water lying around, so your number one priority is to preserve water—stay in the shade and try not to do too much unless you have a plan. If your own supplies are running low, you need to find a decent and plentiful source of water. If you know where—and how—to look, you can find these even in a desert. Look for the clues.

Water detective

WATER BELOW

Although valleys, gullies, and riverbeds may look dry, there will often be water beneath the surface, especially at the outsides of dry river bends and wherever you see green plants growing. Dig a hole and let it fill with water. Empty out the first, dirtiest holeful of water and let it refill. Try lining the hole with stones to keep the water clean.

FOLLOW THE ANIMALS

Desert animals will be regular visitors to reliable sources of water, so look out for fresh animal droppings and animal trails (especially ones coming together or which all lead in the same direction).

Tell-tale poop

Tracks to water

I HAVE A DRINKING PROBLEM—I CAN'T GET ENOUGH

BIRDS

Desert birds drink early in the morning or late in the day; if you see some flying past they may be on their way toward water, or if they are flying low they might be on their way back with heavy bellies full of water.

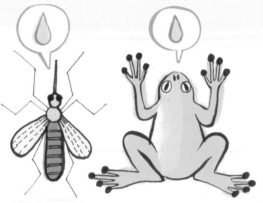

Bee: Usually within 2.5 miles (4km)

Mosquito: Usually within 1,600 feet (500m)

Frog: Usually in the immediate vicinity

CRITTERS

These creatures don't stray far from water. If you see a fly, you are probably within half an hour's walk of water. If you see a mosquito, you must be very close. Ants climbing up a tree may be heading toward a small pool of water that has collected in the branches.

If there's no puddle, get digging!

DRINK WITH CARE

Remember that desert water will often be dirty and even poisonous, so you may need to filter and purify it. In the desert, a simple method of purifying is to leave a clear plastic bottle of water in direct sunlight for several hours.

It will take two days to purify the water during very cloudy conditions.

CLIFFS

When rain falls, some of will it soak into the ground. Some of this may reappear as a spring, often at the base of a cliff. In very sheltered spots, you may even find puddles left over from the last time it rained.

THIRST QUENCHERS

Explorers know how to get the most out of nature, and even in the desert there are lots of natural resources. Desert plants have evolved all sorts of clever ways of finding and storing water, but if you want to take advantage, you need to know which ones to tap and which ones to toss.

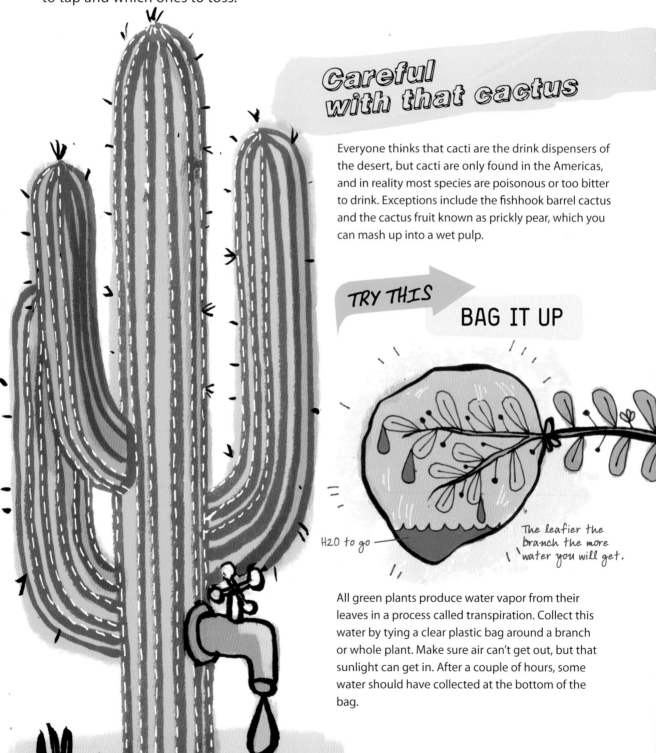

Careful with that cactus

Everyone thinks that cacti are the drink dispensers of the desert, but cacti are only found in the Americas, and in reality most species are poisonous or too bitter to drink. Exceptions include the fishhook barrel cactus and the cactus fruit known as prickly pear, which you can mash up into a wet pulp.

TRY THIS

BAG IT UP

H2O to go

The leafier the branch the more water you will get.

All green plants produce water vapor from their leaves in a process called transpiration. Collect this water by tying a clear plastic bag around a branch or whole plant. Make sure air can't get out, but that sunlight can get in. After a couple of hours, some water should have collected at the bottom of the bag.

SOLAR STILL

TRY THIS

A solar or desert still is a way to use the heat of the sun to get moisture out of the ground. It also gets water out of any plants you can find, and from salty water such as your own pee. Dig a hole and place a bucket in the middle. Fix a clear plastic sheet over a hole in the ground and weigh it with a rock so the sheet bulges down over the bucket. The sun heats the air under the sheet, evaporating water from the ground and whatever else you put in, which then condenses on the underside of the sheet and drips into the bucket.

Warning! Many experts think the amount of water you can get from a desert still is less than the sweat you lose digging it out.

WET, WET, WET

To survive the intense heat of the desert you need to drink up to four times as much water as normal—perhaps a quarter of a gallon an hour during the day, which is equivalent to guzzling three cans of soda every hour for eight hours!

MEET THE LOCALS

TUAREG, BLUE PEOPLE OF THE SAHARA

The Tuareg are nomadic people who live in the Sahara region. They are known as "the people of the veil," because of the traditional face-covering tagelmust, or headscarf, worn by all men over 25, and "the blue people," because the indigo dye from the tagelmust stains their skin. The Tuareg travel across vast areas to find enough food and water; they are brilliant at navigating poop between oases, and are master camel herders. They use every part of the camel, including its dung, which is vital as fuel for fires because there is very little wood in the desert.

I'M FEELING A BIT BLUE

Don't try setting fire to camel poop before it's dry.

DESERT DANGERS

The desert is beautiful but deadly, and an explorer needs more than a big bottle of water to survive and discover. Danger lurks over every dune, from the stinging scorpion to the mysteries of the mirage.

Sandstorms— death from above

A sandstorm is a cloud of dust and sand picked up by a strong wind, which blows across the desert like a giant scouring pad. Sandstorms can kill by choking you, and the fast moving grains of sand can hurt or blind you. If you see one approaching take shelter in a building or vehicle if possible. Close all the doors and windows. If you're on your own, put on goggles and tie a scarf or wet cloth over your face; try to find a rock to shelter behind, curl up into a ball, and cover your head. Camels simply close their eyes and nostrils and wait out the storm—if you know a friendly camel get it to "koosh" (see page 43), and use it as a windbreak.

Pack swimming goggles and a scarf if you are exploring a region where dust storms are likely.

Mirage—tricks of the eye

A mirage is an optical illusion, caused by hot air near the desert surface bending light from the sky. When you see what looks like water in the distance, what you are really seeing is the sky. Don't be fooled!

Scorpions—small but deadly

Related to spiders, scorpions are fearsome-looking with their poisonous stinger, but are mostly harmless. However, there are some scorpions that can be deadly, especially to children. How can you tell which ones are dangerous? Look out for small, straw colored scorpions with long, thin tails—these are the worst. Scorpions generally want to stay away from you, so if you see one give it some room to escape. In the cold desert night they might crawl into boots, hats, backpacks, or even sleeping bags looking for warmth, so make sure you shake everything out carefully in the morning.

Sunstroke—brain boiling

Heatstroke or sunstroke is what happens when your body absorbs heat faster than it can get rid of it. In the fierce sunlight and heat of the desert, it is probably the greatest danger facing the explorer. Try to avoid sunstroke by keeping your head covered at all times (see pages 44–45). Wear loose clothing, but do not take your clothes off. Stay in the shade, and don't do anything during the heat of the day; exploring is for the early morning, evening, and—if the Moon is full—the night time. If you get dizzy or have a headache, stop whatever you are doing and lie down in the shade. Soak your head covering in water, and sip water slowly but continuously.

ALL ABOARD THE SHIP OF THE DESERT

Camels are amazing creatures; they can go without water for more than ten times longer than you can, and when they fill up, they drink up to 40 gallons (150l) at once (enough to kill you several times over). A camel is essential for any serious desert explorer. It can lug your water and tent, provide shade from the sun, shelter from sandstorms and warmth at night, and carry you places even a 4WD vehicle could never reach.

WHY DO CAMELS HAVE HUMPS?

The hump is where the camel stores its fat—in one place rather than spread over the body where it would cause overheating.

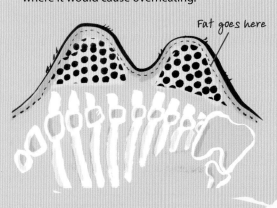

Fat goes here

EYES AND HOOFS

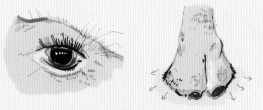

Camels have thorn-proof mouths and sideways opening eyelids that work like windshield wipers to clear out dust. Their feet are webbed to stop them from sinking into the dunes, and they can shut their nostrils to keep out sand.

How to tame a wild camel

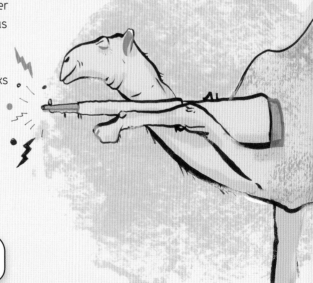

KOOSH

1 Round up some wild camels and put them together in a fenced yard. Pick your camel with care. A two- to three-year-old female is best. Avoid angry-looking males.

2 Use a "coach" camel to help. Having a coach camel that is already tame and trained will reassure and calm the wild camel.

3 Let your camel get used to you. Eventually, she will be comfortable with your presence and touch, especially if you bribe her with food and salt-licks.

4 A halter is what you use to guide the camel around, and, eventually, to ride it. Start by getting the camel used to having a rope over and then around her neck. Then train her to move her head and then her whole body in response to pressure on the halter ropes.

5 Koosh train your camel. "Koosh" is the command you give to a camel to make her kneel down so you can get on.

6 It's time to ride your camel! When you get on the kooshing camel, wrap your legs around the saddle horn. Get ready to be tipped at an alarming angle when she gets up on her hind legs and then front legs.

HARRY THE HORRIBLE

Harry was the first ever camel in Australia, brought over from the Canary Islands in 1840. Six years later, he was recruited by explorer John Ainsworth Horrocks for an expedition into the Outback, but it didn't work out for either of them. While exploring a dried up lake, Horrocks stopped to shoot a bird, but as he was loading his gun Harry lurched sideways and his saddle caught on the trigger. The gun went off, blasting Horrocks in the jaw. The unfortunate explorer died of infection three weeks later, but got his revenge by giving orders for Harry to be shot! Bad-tempered Harry managed to bite his executioner on the hand before the deed was done.

Never put your face in the way of a loaded (or unloaded) gun!

WHERE DID YOU GET THAT HAT?

Dressing up is half the fun of being an explorer, and the desert doesn't disappoint. Wearing the right thing on your head will save your life—but what is the right thing? It depends who you want to copy. Do you see yourself as a member of the French Foreign Legion, or would you prefer to be a desert tribesman, like the Tuareg (see page 39)?

Cork hat

Remove bottles first.

In the Australian outback, thirsty flies try to get into your mouth, nose, and eyes to get a drink. The solution to this pesky problem is the cork hat. The corks swing around as you move to stop the flies from landing.

Tagelmust

Indigo dye is made from soaked and fermented leaves.

A tagelmust is a scarf that winds around the head and covers the face, so that a single piece of cloth can protect you from the sun, and keep out sand and dust. The Tuareg wear blue tagelmust, while Bedouin often wear a black one. Dark colors screen out harmful sunlight, like sunglasses for your head, but they also soak up the light more. The best combination is probably a dark cloth covered with a light, white cloth.

Cap and cloth

If you have to improvise, tuck a cloth into the headband of an ordinary cap to create a DIY kepi. You can even make use of your urine by peeing on the neck cloth, so that it cools you as it evaporates in the desert heat.

WARNING
You may end up smelling worse than your camel!

The back of your neck needs shade too.

French kepi

I DARE YOU TO LAUGH AT MY HAT!

Foreign Legionnaires wear hats called kepis. The brim shades the eyes (and adds a touch of military style), while the high boxy part captures an insulating pocket of air. A cloth down the back shades the neck and ears.

Safari hat

Wide brim

This favorite item of African exploration is made from cork or pith—a spongy plant material that can be pressed into almost any shape. The safari hat lets air through, which helps to keep your head cool.

SAND DUNES

Desert dunes are created by windblown sand. The shape a dune takes depends on the prevailing wind direction and the amount of sand there is to blow around.

Star—Where winds come from three or more different directions, star dunes form.

Parabolic—The horns of these U-shaped dunes point upwind.

Linear—These dunes form parallel to the average wind direction where sand is plentiful.

Barchan—The crescent-shaped dunes with horns pointing downwind form where wind direction is constant but sand supply is limited.

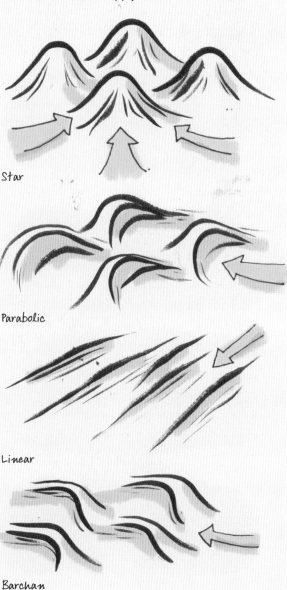

Star

Parabolic

Linear

Barchan

DRASTIC MEASURES

The desert is a harsh and potentially dangerous environment. For safety's sake, it's best to travel there in a group, and you should always have an escape plan if things go wrong. Aron Ralston went into the desert alone. When he got stuck, he thought of an escape plan—but it wasn't an easy one.

GIVE THE MAN A HAND: THE ARON RALSTON STORY

In April 2003 Aron Ralston was exploring Bluejohn Canyon, in the Utah desert, when he slipped and fell down a crevasse. The fall dislodged a boulder, which pinned his hand to the wall. It was impossible to free his hand or move the rock, and Ralston hadn't told anyone where he was going, so he knew there would be no one to help him. After six days, suffering from dehydration and low body temperature, he decided to amputate his own hand, using a blunt multi-tool he had with him. After cutting off his hand, he lowered himself to the floor of the canyon and walked to safety.

Don't get stuck in a pickle like Aron. Always tell someone where you're going and when you'll be back.

Ouch!
Extreme First Aid

Aron Ralston isn't the only explorer who has had to do something really painful when there has been no one around to help. All of the things on this page have been done at some time by somebody stuck in the wilderness. While it's important to learn some basic first aid, definitely leave these medical procedures to someone who knows what they are doing.

GLOBE LUXATION

This is the fancy medical term for when your eyeball pops out of your head. Happily, this will almost certainly never happen to you, but it can occur if you are poked in the eye in exactly the right (or wrong) way. To return the eyeball to its proper place, push gently on the white bits of the eye with clean fingers.

SUTURE

These stitches hold the sides of a wound together to help it heal. They sting going in and they sting coming out.

TOOTH EXTRACTION

Almost nothing hurts as much as a toothache—just ask one of the many explorers who have decided to tear out a tooth rather than put up with an aching one for a minute longer. It helps to have a pair of pliers and a strong arm.

APPENDECTOMY

One morning in April 1961, at a remote Antarctic scientific base, Leonid Rogozov began to feel very ill. All his symptoms indicated that his appendix had burst— he had to be operated on or he would surely die. One problem though—he was the only doctor at the base and he would have to operate on himself! Fortunately he had some local anaesthetic available and some friends to assist (although they almost fainted).

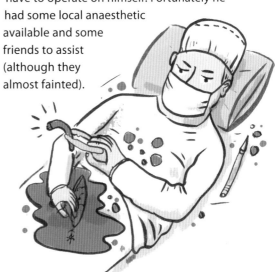

TRACHEOTOMY

A tracheotomy is a little hole cut in the throat that allows a person to breathe when their airway isn't working. It can be the only way to save a person's life if they have a serious throat injury or an obstruction that can't be removed. The hole needs to be kept open. The body of a pen or a drinking straw can help.

The Arctic tern migrates from the Arctic to Antarctica every year.

Antarctica is the best place to look for meteorites—they are easy to see on the snow.

Learn to drive a dog sled. See pages 56-57.

Seals live in both the Arctic and Antarctic, plus many other parts of the world.

Polar bears and walrus live in the Arctic.

Penguins live in the southern hemisphere only. They don't have to worry about polar bears.

POLAR

According to your GPS tracker you are just a two-day hike from the Pole, but things aren't going well. The food for the dogs ran out two days ago; you could butcher one of them to feed to the others, or maybe try producing one of their favorite delicacies—human poop. Now a blizzard is closing in—when the short day ends the temperature will drop to 70 below. Should you press on, turn back, or try to build a shelter using nothing but snow and a shovel?

Amundsen-Scott South Pole Station.

EXPLORER'S QUEST

The ultimate ends of Earth are the absolute limit of human exploration, and true explorers are always looking to push themselves to the limit. Icy deserts, frozen seas, impenetrable mountains, savage bears, and less savage penguins protect the secrets of the Polar regions. What will you discover at the top or bottom of the planet?

Race to the Pole

Unfortunately, you've missed your chance to become the first person to reach either the North or South Pole. Although you may be joining this race a little late, the contest to see who can reach the North and South Poles in the most challenging ways possible continues. Perhaps you could be the first person to walk to the South Pole backward, or the first person to kayak to the North Pole—if the ice cap keeps melting?

IF I WAS AT THE NORTH POLE, I'D BE ON MY FEET!

Mountains at the end of the world

The most remote and unexplored mountains on Earth are the Transantarctic Mountains, a range 2,000 miles (3,200km) long and 14,800 feet (4,500m) high that cuts across the polar continent. All the great Antarctic adventurers explored these mountains, but they still hold many secrets—perhaps you could scuba dive in a lake that has been frozen over for millions of years, or look for water in the Dry Valleys, one of the driest environments on Earth?

The Northwest Passage

A way for ships to sail from the Atlantic to the Pacific, across the top of North America, was the Holy Grail for Arctic explorers for centuries. In fact, there is a sea passage through the islands of the Canadian Arctic Archipelago, but much of it is choked with ice for most of the year. Today less ice forms every year, so there is a greater chance than ever that you could open up a Northwest Passage for the ships of the world.

It's still a cold part of the world so keep an eye out for icebergs.

THE LOST EXPEDITION

In 1845, Sir John Franklin set off into the icy waters of the Canadian Arctic Archipelago to search for the Northwest Passage (see above), but he vanished, along with his two ships and all 127 of his party. A few bodies and artifacts have been found, but the whereabouts of his ships, and most importantly, his expedition logs (notes telling the story of the expedition), are still unknown—can you find them?

If Franklin had asked the Inuit for help, he might have lived a bit longer.

MEET THE LOCALS

INUIT

Anyone who goes exploring at the Poles must learn the ways and wisdom of the Inuit, or face certain death. The Inuit are the native peoples of the Canadian and Greenland Arctic. They used to be called Eskimos, but this was a name given to them by outsiders. They prefer the word Inuit, which means "human beings."

INUIT TECHNOLOGY

The Inuit have become experts at making a little go a long way. They make clothes and equipment better than anything that outsiders could invent (until relatively recently), so the best polar explorers copied the Inuit. For instance, the American explorer Robert Peary had a team of Inuit women who made clothes especially for him and each of his men.

GET YOUR OWN COAT, IT TOOK ME AGES TO GROW MINE

An average polar bear skin yielded three pairs of trousers and one pair of boots.

SNOW GOGGLES *TRY THIS*

Sunlight reflecting from snow can quickly blind you. The Inuit used to make snow goggles by taking strips of caribou antler and cutting slits in them. You can make something similar using cardboard roll. Cut it open, flatten it out, and slice a rectangle big enough to cover your eyes, then hold it up to your face and get someone to mark the position of your eyes and nose. Cut a notch for your nose and narrow rectangular slits for your eyes. Punch a hole at each end to hold rubber bands big enough to stretch over your ears and keep the goggles in place.

INSTANT SNOWSHOE

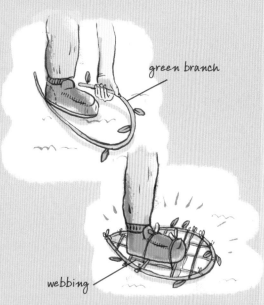

green branch

webbing

Walking in snow will quickly tire you out. Use snowshoes to spread your weight so you can walk on top of the snow. In an emergency, make your own snowshoes by bending a green branch or sapling into a hoop (like a tennis racket), and using more saplings to make a web, or simply strap a branch from a fir tree to your boots.

MIND YOUR MANNERS

Explorers must learn the customs and manners of the locals. For instance, did you know that offering a lift on your sled used to be a way of asking an Inuit girl to marry you? Inuit eat a lot of their meat raw—they especially like raw seal tongue, brain, and eyes—and if you don't want to upset them you'd better join in.

Cooking these won't make them any more appetizing, so you might as well eat them raw.

HOME SWEET DOME

After a hard day's walking or sledding across the ice, you need somewhere to rest and stay warm. And when a polar storm or blizzard arrives, you'd better take shelter, or you will soon freeze to death. The Inuit came up with one of the best and simplest ideas—use snow to make a little house that keeps heat inside and won't blow away in the wind: an igloo.

How to build an igloo

1 Mark a circle on the ground, about 6.5 feet (2m) across. Stamp down the snow inside the circle until is hard.

3 Lay the first row of blocks in a circle. Use your saw to cut a ramp in them.

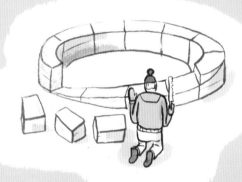

2 Use your saw to cut blocks of hard snow (you may have to dig down to find it). First, cut two parallel lines, then make a horizontal cut, and lastly, make a vertical cut.

4 Now lay blocks in a spiral around the ramp. Trim the sides of the blocks so that as you go up they slant inward. The last block should sit in the hole at the top, and should be wider at the top so it is held in place.

5 On the side facing away from the wind, dig down to make an entrance. Use two slabs of hard snow to make a little roof.

6 A proper igloo has a raised platform around one side, to make a seat/sleeping area.

If you use a stove, make sure you make a chimney, or invisible fumes might kill you.

EXPLORING MISTAKES

Learn from the mistakes of past explorers. When the Duke of Abruzzi went to Alaska in 1897 he took several iron beds with him, as he was too posh to sleep on the floor. In fact air circulates under a raised bed, so it is warmer to sleep on the floor. Also, remember to bring stuff inside your shelter! When a storm buried his tent in snow, British polar explorer Augustine Courthauld was unable to dig himself out for *six weeks* because he had left his shovel outside.

I SHOULD HAVE BROUGHT A HEATING PAD

THE POLAR EXPRESS

Walking on snow and ice in the freezing cold burns up so much energy that you can effectively starve to death in a few days even though you are eating what seem like normal portions. The Inuit long ago learned to use man's best friend to give themselves an easier ride.

Dog driving

Driving a team of dogs while riding a sled is not easy. The traces (the ropes that hold the dogs together and attach them to the sled) get easily tangled, and the dogs fight and may become lazy if not properly commanded. Your sled should have a handlebar, skis or runners, and a brake.

1. Keep your foot hard on the brake until you are ready.
2. Ease off on the brake and give the "go" command (such as "Mush!").
3. Brace yourself for a jerk when you start off.
4. You may need to push with one foot, as though you were on a scooter, to get the dogs going.
5. Keep some pressure on the brake until the dogs have pulled the lines taut.

DOGS DINNER

In 1911, Amundsen and Scott raced to reach the South Pole (see pages 60-61). Amundsen beat Scott and made it back alive. One reason was that he used dogs, whereas Scott hated using dog-sleds, so he traveled on foot. Sled dogs, or huskies, are strong and light, making them perfect for traveling on snow and ice. They eat meat, so you can hunt for their food as you travel instead of having to bring it with you. In extreme circumstances, you can even feed them to each other. They also like to eat human poop!

TIME TO GET OUT AND PUSH

The dogs' dinner— make it meaty.

Handle bar

Runner

Cargo and cover

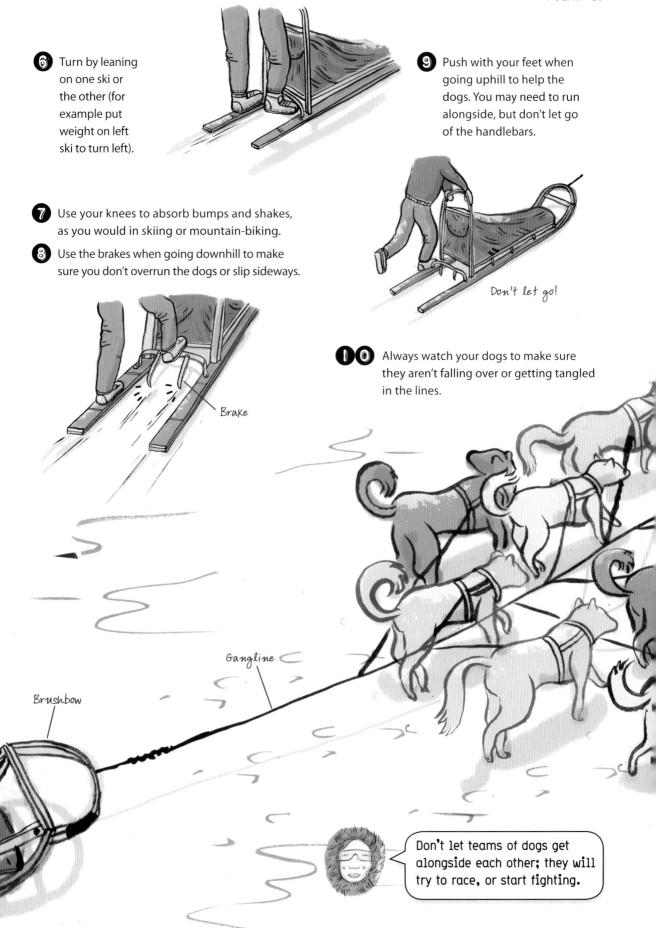

6 Turn by leaning on one ski or the other (for example put weight on left ski to turn left).

7 Use your knees to absorb bumps and shakes, as you would in skiing or mountain-biking.

8 Use the brakes when going downhill to make sure you don't overrun the dogs or slip sideways.

Brake

9 Push with your feet when going uphill to help the dogs. You may need to run alongside, but don't let go of the handlebars.

Don't let go!

10 Always watch your dogs to make sure they aren't falling over or getting tangled in the lines.

Gangline

Brushbow

Don't let teams of dogs get alongside each other; they will try to race, or start fighting.

BEARS AND BITES

Arctic explorers have to worry about two kinds of bites: bear bites and frost bite. At least in the Antarctic there are no bears!

Survive a polar bear attack

Bears are huge and dangerous, but at least most species of bear will avoid you if given the chance. Polar bears—the biggest land carnivores on Earth—are different; they will hunt humans, especially if they are hungry.

- If you see a polar bear in the distance, move off in the opposite direction. But don't run; back away slowly.

- If one comes toward you, put your hands up in the air and shout and stamp. Sound an air horn if you have one. This will make you look bigger, and could make the bear change its mind.

- The best defense against an attacking polar bear is a big gun, but you could try bear spray (pepper spray).

Frostbite

Frostbite is when the blood stops flowing to a part of the body and it freezes. If one of your toes freezes and then thaws out, it won't come back to life; it is now dead, and will start rotting. It will also be incredibly painful. The parts of the body most at risk of frostbite are the toes and feet, fingers and hands, and the nose. If you don't want to lose some or all of these, be careful!

- Keep everything covered with the right sort of gloves and boots; warm and not too tight.

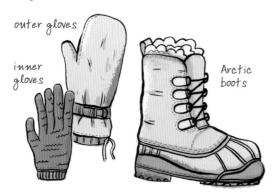

outer gloves

inner gloves

Arctic boots

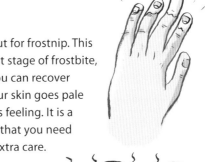

- Watch out for frostnip. This is the first stage of frostbite, which you can recover from; your skin goes pale and loses feeling. It is a warning that you need to take extra care.

- Keep dry. The biggest danger is when your socks or gloves get wet and then freeze. Change your socks often if you need to; dry out wet socks by putting them inside your pants.

- If your feet get really badly frostbitten, you are probably better off leaving them frozen. If they thaw out they will become incredibly painful, but if they stay cold you can still walk on the frozen stumps.

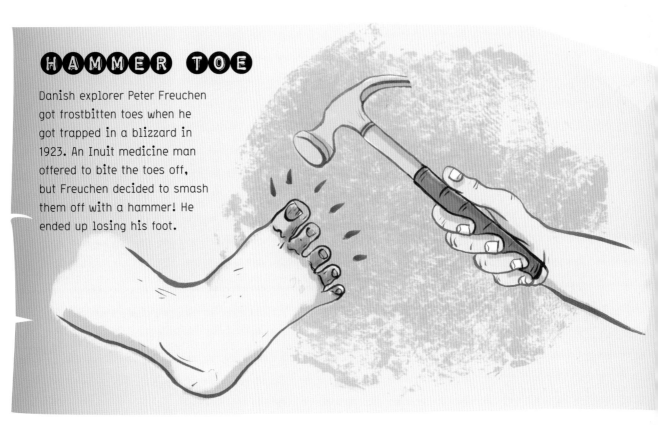

HAMMER TOE

Danish explorer Peter Freuchen got frostbitten toes when he got trapped in a blizzard in 1923. An Inuit medicine man offered to bite the toes off, but Freuchen decided to smash them off with a hammer! He ended up losing his foot.

RACE TO THE POLE

The three greatest names in Antarctic exploration are probably Robert Falcon Scott, Ernest Shackleton, and Roald Amundsen. Their successes and disasters offer valuable lessons for trainee explorers.

Scott of the Antarctic

Scott was heroically brave, but he made many terrible mistakes. He refused to learn how to use dogs, and tried instead to use ponies. He and his men mostly hauled their own sleds. His attempt to reach the Pole involved a complicated plan, and he was not as thorough or professional in his preparations as his rival Amundsen. Although Scott made it to the Pole, he was beaten there by Amundsen, and he and all his men died on the way back to base.

Bubble burst

The most modern equipment is no good without a decent plan. In 1897, explorer Salomon Andrée set off for the North Pole using all the latest technology, including a hydrogen balloon and remote-controlled stove. But the balloon didn't work properly in the freezing air; Andrée and his crew crashed not far from where they started, and were eaten by bears!

Will your equipment work the way you expect in extreme environments?

Shackleton's endurance

In 1914, Ernest Shackleton set out to reach Antarctica, intending to cross from coast to coast, but disaster struck when his ship, the *Endurance*, was trapped in the ice. Eventually the ship was crushed and Shackleton had to lead his crew onto the ice, and then to a small island. The only hope of rescue was to reach the whaling station on South Georgia Island, 800 miles (1,500km) away, in a small lifeboat. Shackleton made it, and eventually every one of his men was rescued.

The key to Shackleton's success was leadership. He treated his men well, making time to chat with them. A badly led team is a recipe for disaster.

Amundsen the airman

Roald Amundsen was the first to reach the South Pole, and managed to get there and back without losing any men or dogs. His success was down to his ruthlessness, careful planning, and attention to detail. Amundsen later became interested in flying, and made the first trans-Arctic flight, but he died in 1928 when his airplane crashed while he was helping search for survivors of an airship disaster. It was probably the only time he hadn't prepared properly.

Train thoroughly, choose the right equipment, and have a simple and well-thought out plan.

Avoid avalanches.
See pages 76-77.

FOREST & MOUNTAIN

The mountain peak is hidden by clouds. If you wait for it to clear before trying to reach the summit, the hot sun will set loose a rain of killer boulders and deadly avalanches, but since you spent the night in a bivvy bag hanging off a vertical cliff face, above a thousand-foot drop to a forest filled with hungry wolves and fierce bears, it would help to see where you are going. On top of all this, you need to go to the bathroom, and your zipper is stuck. Should you take off your gloves to jiggle it, or rub a pencil on the zipper?

Beware the bears!
See page 67.

EXPLORER'S QUEST

With forests covering their lower slopes, and sharp peaks jutting into the sky, the mountain ranges of the world attract a very special type of explorer. The type willing to dodge bears and wolves, and brave the terrors of the death zone, so that they can be the first person to stand on top of a mountain. However, claiming the first ascent is not the only challenge for explorers in the forest and mountain zone.

Climb an unclimbed monster

Believe it or not, there are lots of mountains in the world that no one has ever climbed. Some of them are almost as high as Mount Everest! You could write your name in the history books by being the first person to get to the top of one of these unclimbed monsters, but you will need to travel somewhere remote, like Greenland or eastern Tibet.

Circumnavigate the taiga belt

The taiga is the immense forest that runs in a belt around the top of the Earth. Pick the right route and you could circumnavigate (travel all the way around) the globe almost without leaving the forest, but would you be able to cope with bears, wolves, and intense cold without losing your way?

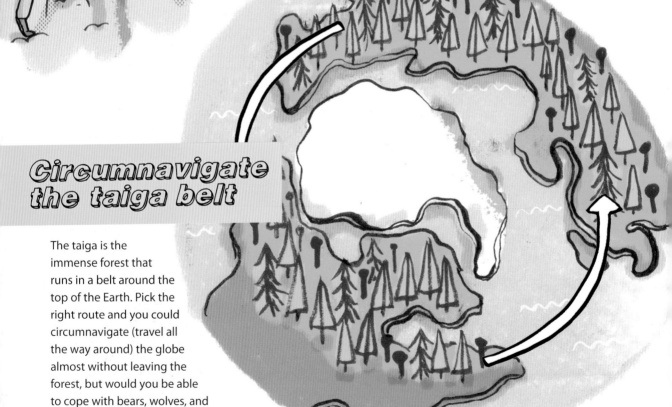

MYSTERY OF MALLORY AND IRVINE'S CAMERA

George Mallory and Sandy Irvine died in 1924 trying to make the first ascent of Everest (see page 82). No one knows whether they made it to the top before they perished, but the mystery could be solved if Irvine's body is found, and with it the camera he was carrying which might contain images of the men at the summit. Can you solve the greatest mystery of mountain exploration by tracking down a body lost for nearly a century and recovering an antique camera?

Find the Yeti

The people of the Himalayas speak of an ape-like beast who lurks among the snowy peaks. Many visiting explorers have seen footprints or claim to have spotted the creature. Can you find proof that the Yeti or Abominable Snowman is real?

Track down a living fossil

Hidden away in the mountain ranges of the world are some very special places—isolated valleys where ancient forests still grow. In these unique spots, trees are able to survive the passing of ice ages, and even the passing of the dinosaurs. Trees like the 40,000-year-old grove of quaking aspens found in Utah, or the Wollemi Pines of Australia's Blue Mountains that until their discovery in 1994 were known only through fossils. Can you penetrate the deep mountains and discover the living remnants of a prehistoric forest?

BIG BAD BEASTS

Since the first humans left Africa and started to move through the endless forests of the northern world, explorers have battled with terrifying beasts among the trees. Today there are far fewer big predators of all kinds, including bears and wolves, but if you get lost in a wilderness area you still run the risk of becoming food for a hungry animal.

When wolf packs attack

WANT A BITE?

Wolves live and hunt in packs, and they are cunning and dangerous predators. They very rarely attack humans, but if you are alone in a remote place, especially in winter when food is scarce and the wolves are hungry, they may start to hunt you. Here's how to survive a wolf attack.

- Do not look a wolf in the eye or show your teeth. This looks aggressive and might prompt it to attack.

- Don't run; the wolf will chase you, and a wolf can run much faster than you.

- Get on top of a rock or climb a tree if possible.

- Stand up tall and make yourself look as big as possible. Hold your backpack or wave your arms above your head.

- If a wolf attacks, fight back! Aim for the nose. Protect your throat and face with your forearm. If all else fails, ram your hand down its throat.

Bear necessities

Black bear

Front track

Hind track

Front track

Hind track

Brown bear

Bears come in different varieties. Polar bears are the most dangerous (see page 58), but in the forest or mountains you could meet brown or black bears. Black bears are smaller and less dangerous. Brown bears, especially the type known as grizzly bears, are big and very dangerous, but even they generally prefer not to attack humans. The greatest danger comes from bumping into one, so that it feels cornered, or from a bear being attracted by the smell of your food. To avoid a bear attack, make a lot of noise as you walk and keep your food "bear safe" (see below). Never get between a mother and her cubs. If you see a baby bear, start backing away and go back the way you came.

Always keep your food out of reach of bears. Try tying your food stores to a line, then suspend it between two trees at least 12 feet (3.5m) above the ground.

Bear attack!

If you come face to face with a bear...

1 Don't look it in the eye—turn slightly sideways.

2 Do not run! Bears can run faster than you.

3 If the bear is coming for you, stand up straight and wave your hands over your head, yelling and screeching.

4 If the bear still attacks, fall face down on the ground with your fingers locked around your neck and play dead.

5 If the bear starts biting you, stab it in the eyes or mouth with a knife, or squirt bear spray in its eyes.

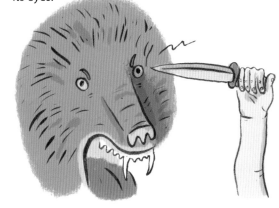

FRUITS OF THE FOREST

The forest can be frightening, but it is also one of the friendliest places to go exploring, because you can find a fantastic range of things to eat, if you know how and where to look. Explorers like to travel light, so living off the land is an essential skill to learn.

Forest feast

So, what's on the menu? There are 120,000 types of plant in the world that you can eat, and many of them can be found in the forest. Look for the fruits, berries, nuts, seeds, and roots of plants—these are the parts with all the good stuff. But beware— there are also lots of poisonous plants, so you need to be careful and make sure you know something is safe before you gobble it. Never eat anything unless you are certain it won't harm you!

AVOID

- Mushrooms and toadstools unless you are an expert and know which ones are safe.
- Anything from a plant with milky white sap.
- Anything from a red or white plant or a plant covered with fine hairs or spines.
- White or yellow berries.

Mushrooms and toadstools

Trees with milky sap

LIKELY TO BE SAFE

- Plants growing in wet soil or in the water.
- Roots, bulbs, and tubers (but always cook them first to destroy any poison).
- Ferns.
- Blue and black berries.
- Berries that have lots of little bits joined together (like a raspberry or blackberry).
- Grass seeds (but don't eat them if there are little black bits growing out of them).

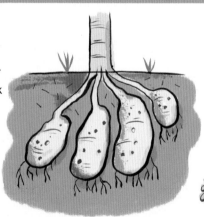

Roots, bulbs and, tubers

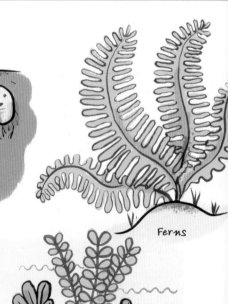

Ferns

Plants growing in water

If you get the chance, watch wild animals like deer and boar to see where they are looking for nuts and roots.

Bug out

It might sound yucky, but insects, worms, slugs, and other creepy crawlies are good to eat. Bite the heads off insect larvae before swallowing them, and drop worms into water before chomping on them.

Red or white plants   White berries

Blue and black berries

Grass seeds

Fishy business —DIY fish trap

Mountains and forests are usually wet, which means lots of rivers and streams. Freshwater fish make for great eating. A good way to catch them is to make a simple fish trap. You can make one at home, and try catching a fish in your nearest stream (so long as fishing is allowed there).

1 Cut the top off a large plastic bottle, about a third of the way up.

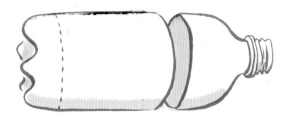

2 Put some bait in the bottom part—you could use a worm or insect.

3 Turn the top half around and stick it into the bottom half. Make sure the cap is off!

4 When a fish swims through the narrow neck of the bottle to get the bait, it won't be able to find its way out again.

5 Put the bottle in the stream in a good spot— at the outside of a bend, in the shade of the overhanging bank. Keep it in place with rocks and sticks.

MEET THE LOCALS

• •

SHERPAS

The Sherpas are people from Nepal who have special mountaineering abilities: they are amazingly strong, can carry extremely heavy loads for a long time, and they don't suffer from the same health problems that affect most people when they get too high up (see page 79). Many Sherpas are also brilliant climbers, and almost all expeditions to Everest and other nearby Himalayan mountains use Sherpas as guides and porters (people who carry stuff).

ENOUGH YAKETY-YAK, LET'S GET CLIMBING!

TEA AND YAK MILK

There are around 30,000 Sherpas in Nepal. To the Nepalese "Sherpa" means "people from the east," but they originally came from Tibet. Most Sherpas still live traditional lives; herding yaks (animals like very hairy cows with big horns), which help them carry heavy loads and provide milk, meat, wool and dung for making fires. The Sherpas' favorite meal is shyakpa (a meat and potato stew), and they drink tea mixed with yak butter and salt.

GODS OF THE MOUNTAIN

The Sherpas call Mount Everest *Chomolungma* or "Goddess Mother of the Land." They believe it is the home of the gods, a place where humans were not allowed to go. European explorers changed their minds, but today it is still important to start any climb on Everest with a special Sherpa ceremony called a Puja, where you offer gifts to the gods so that they will help you get to the top.

Nepalese prayer flags traditionally come in five colors: blue, white, red, green, and yellow.

THE HIGH LIFE

Sherpas live in mountain villages. Some of these villages are over 13,000 feet (4,000m) up—that's more than ten times higher than the Empire State Building. Most people in the world would get a headache just visiting these villages. There are no roads or cars up on the mountains, so Sherpas have to carry everything themselves—even televisions and refrigerators. Some Sherpa kids have to climb 1,500 feet (450m) to get to school, which is like going up 150 stories to attend class!

UP, UP, AND AWAY

The two most important and useful things for climbing a snowy or icy mountain are rope and an ice axe. Knowing how to use these can get you to the top of a mountain no one has ever been up before, and could save your life in case you start coming down faster than you want to.

Ice axe to the rescue

An ice axe is more like a pick or hammer—the head of the axe has both a blunt and a spiky end, and the bottom of the shaft is also pointy. All these parts can be used to stick the axe into the snow or ice, giving you something to hold onto. The ice axe is also used for chipping out footholds in the ice, and for carving a snow cave if you need to take shelter. When you are walking up a snowy slope, with every step, push the shaft of the axe into the snow up the slope from where you are standing. If you start to slip you can put one hand on the head and push down, and hold the bottom of the shaft with the other hand. This is called a self-belay.

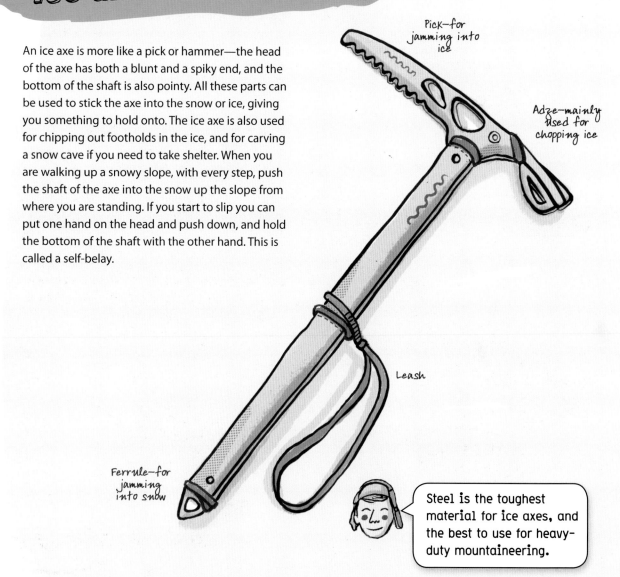

Pick—for jamming into ice

Adze—mainly used for chopping ice

Leash

Ferrule—for jamming into snow

Steel is the toughest material for ice axes, and the best to use for heavy-duty mountaineering.

Self-arrest

The ice axe can save your life if you start to slide down a slope, using a technique called self-arrest. You need to practice this before trying to climb Everest. The aim is to end up on your stomach with your feet pointing downhill and the head of your ice axe buried in the snow.

1 Stay calm—hurtling down a slope toward a cliff or sharp rocks is pretty terrifying, but if you stay calm you can survive.

2 Hold onto the ice axe with both hands.

THIS IS SNOW FUN AT ALL!

3 Stick the pick part of the ice axe into the snow on one side of your body.

4 Use the pick as a pivot point and swing round onto your front, until you are on your front and your feet are pointing downhill.

5 Arch your body slightly so that your knees and toes are digging in, and so that your weight is pressing the axe into the snow.

MORE NEXT PAGE

Help from your friends

Mountain exploring is best done with at least two people. If you can't find a friend with the same dreams of exploration as you, why not hire a Sherpa to come with you (see pages 70–71)? One reason why you need a companion is so that you can belay your way up a mountain. Belaying is a method of climbing where there is always one person holding a rope tied to the other person so as to catch the climber if he or she falls.

- The first, or lead, climber goes up first, with a rope tied around her waist, and she fixes "protection" (places where the rope can be fixed to the rock) along the way. If she slips and falls, the second climber, or belayer, is holding the rope taut so the lead climber will only fall as far as the first protection.

- Once the lead climber gets to the top of the slope, she fixes the rope to some protection (such as a rock or tree), and the belayer comes up, picking up the protection as he goes. Then they start all over again for the next pitch.

WORK HARD, BELAY HARD

DIY KNOTS

If you are doing anything with a rope, you need to practice your knots. Knots are amazingly useful for the explorer. You need them for everything, from building a raft to crossing a piranha-infested river to fixing a rope bridge across a bottomless chasm. Here are three useful knots you can practise at home.

FIGURE OF EIGHT LOOP

This knot provides a good way to make a loop at one end of a rope, which won't get jammed tight.

1 Loop the rope and bend the looped end (called a "bight") around the double "tail." This creates an eye.

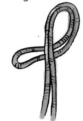

2 Push the bight around the tail and up through the eye.

3 Now you have a strong loop you can put over a branch or into a carabiner.

PRUSIK

A prusik knot slides up and down a rope when unweighted but doesn't slip under a downward force. You can use two prusik knots (one for your feet and another clipped to a harness) to ascend a rope.

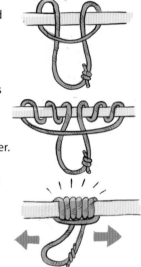

1 Wrap the loop around the rope, and back through itself.

2 Repeat this process twice more so there is a triple loop top and bottom.

3 Push the knot together. It will slide up but will hold when pulled downward.

Prusik cord must have a smaller diameter than the main rope.

DOUBLE FISHERMAN'S

Use this knot to tie two ropes together (for instance, when repairing a rope bridge across a gorge).

1 Lie the ends of the two ropes together.

2 With each rope, make two turns around both ropes, back in the direction of the rest of the rope.

3 Pass the end through the loops and pull each end tight. You should end up with two "x" shapes.

Jungle gorillas sometimes use knots when making their vine beds.

AVALANCHE!

An avalanche is a massive flood of snow traveling at up to 225mph (360km/h), pushing hurricane force winds ahead of it. As a mountain explorer you need to know how to avoid getting hit by an avalanche, and what to do if you can't.

Anatomy of an avalanche

The most dangerous avalanches are dry snow avalanches where a whole slab of snow slips off the mountainside. These generally travel at around 80mph (130km/h), breaking up into chunks and powder as they go. Most people who get killed by an avalanche are walking on the snow slab when it starts sliding, rather than hit by one from above.

ALERT!

Avalanches are most likely to happen when a lot of snow builds up very quickly on a steep slope. So you need to watch out after a heavy storm or snowfall, and especially where the wind has blown snow onto a slope.

Avalanches are more likely to occur on slopes that are being warmed by the sun. In avalanche danger areas move early or wait until the slopes are in the shade. The other big danger is that your weight will make a slab of snow slip. If you step on snow and cracks go out from your foot, you are in danger. Back away from the slope and look for a better route.

Windblown snow equals danger

Avoid sunlit slopes

How to survive an avalanche

1 If you see one coming try to move out of its way, and take shelter behind a rock or tree if possible.

2 If you are caught in the start of one, try to get to the edge of the slide.

3 Cover your mouth so you don't choke on powder snow.

4 While the avalanche is flowing, it behaves like water. Once it stops it will start to get hard and solid. If you get caught in one try to get to the edge using swimming motions, and aim to stay afloat.

5 If you come to a stop underneath the snow, clear a breathing space in front of your face. Do this quickly before the snow sets hard.

6 You will probably be disorientated. Spit or pee to see which way is up—you can tell from the direction the spit or pee is dribbling.

7 You will have to wait for your companions to dig you out. The good news is that the snow is about 70 percent air, but the bad news is that you only have about 20 minutes before the stale air you exhale suffocates you.

ARMED AND DANGEROUS

The 1953 Hunt expedition to Everest was equipped with a mortar (a kind of cannon), so that they could clear away dangerous snow by blasting the slopes with explosives and triggering avalanches. In the end they only used the mortar as a firework launcher.

THE DEATH ZONE

The mountains are full of dangers for explorers, from mountain sickness to crevasses. Worst of all is the "Death Zone," above 26,000 feet (8,000m) in altitude, where the human body cannot survive without help. Every minute you spend in this zone, you are dying.

Cracks of doom

A glacier is a frozen river of ice. High mountains often have glaciers filling their valleys, and you might have to cross one. The ice bends and stretches causing cracks known as crevasses to open up. They can be very narrow but very deep, and what makes them so dangerous is that they can get covered in snow, so you can easily fall in. If you fall in to a crevasse, you probably won't ever come out. It is always best to walk around them unless you are part of an experienced team all roped together. That way if you fall in, your friends can help pull you out again.

If you do fall into a crevasse alone and you survive, it's sometimes better to go down not up, and hope that you can find a way out.

Sick as a dog

Altitude sickness—technically known as acute mountain sickness (AMS)—is what happens when the human body climbs to heights it is not used to. We need oxygen to live, but the higher up you go, the less oxygen there is. In the thin air, you get tired very quickly, you lack energy, you can't think clearly, and you can start seeing and hearing things. You even run the risk of getting a swollen brain, which can easily kill you. To cope with AMS, you need to spend time getting used to high altitudes, moving to higher ground one day at a time.

The best cure for AMS is to head downhill.

MISSION IMPOSSIBLE

To conquer Everest or other mountains over 26,000 feet (8,000m), you need oxygen, unless you can climb quickly enough to get to the top and back down before you die. The first people to climb Everest without oxygen were Reinhold Messner and Peter Habeler in 1978. Early British explorers thought taking oxygen to help you climb was unsporting, and one of the organizers of the 1922 Everest expedition called anyone who used oxygen a "rotter."

OXYGEN IS FOR WIMPS!

At the summit of Everest Messner described himself as "nothing more than a single narrow gasping lung."

HOW TO RAPPEL INTO A VOLCANO

A volcano is a crack in Earth's crust, where hot liquid rock (lava), ash, and gas escape from deep underground. A volcano is an exciting place for an explorer—not only are there many scientific discoveries to be made, there aren't many people who've climbed into a volcano (and even fewer who've climbed out!).

The ring of fire

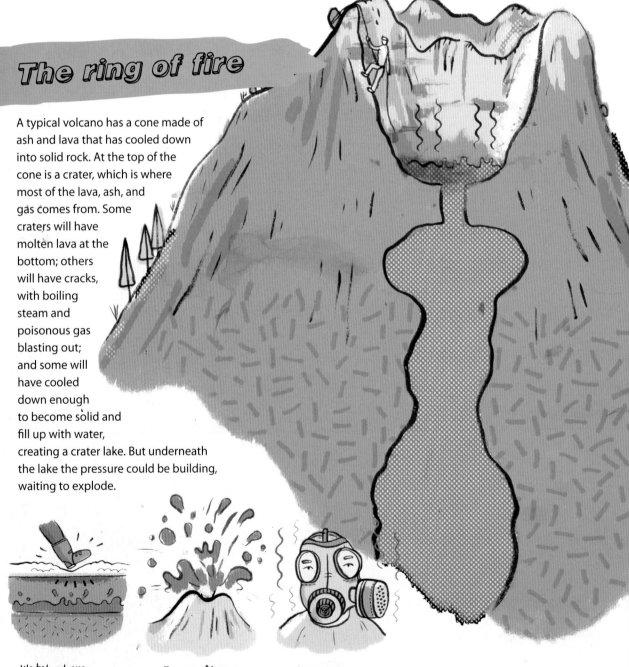

A typical volcano has a cone made of ash and lava that has cooled down into solid rock. At the top of the cone is a crater, which is where most of the lava, ash, and gas comes from. Some craters will have molten lava at the bottom; others will have cracks, with boiling steam and poisonous gas blasting out; and some will have cooled down enough to become solid and fill up with water, creating a crater lake. But underneath the lake the pressure could be building, waiting to explode.

Watch where you step!

Beware flying lava bombs

Gas mask may be required

Rappelling basics

1. You can abseil with nothing more than a long piece of rope—it must be at least twice as long as the cliff you want to go down.

2. Loop it in half and put the loop over something very strong (e.g. a big rock)—this is your anchor point.

3. Face the anchor point and pass the doubled-up rope between your legs and around the back of your right thigh.

4. Pull the rope up across your chest and over your left shoulder, then back down across your back so you can hold it in front of you with your right hand.

5. Carefully walk backward to the edge of the cliff and lean back. Use your right hand to very slowly release the rope. Make sure you are staying right out from the slope as you move down.

6. If you are going too fast bring your right arm around in front of you.

VOLCANO RAPPELLING

You will need proper gear, including a harness and a descender. You should also have heat-proof clothes and boots, and possibly oxygen masks. Test carefully for poisonous gas, and listen to expert advice on whether the volcano is about to blow.

THE MOUTH OF HELL

Mount Erebus in Antarctica is one of the world's most mysterious volcanoes. Shackleton visited it in 1908 and he and his men looked into the crater, which was full of steam. In 1955, there was only solid rock in the crater, but when a team of New Zealand scientists visited in 1974 it was full of lava. They tried rappelling into the crater to collect some molten lava, but the lava lake burped, throwing lava bombs at them. They got out as quick as they could.

Always follow expert advice about whether it is safe to go in the crater.

EXPLORERS ON EVEREST

Everest is a mountain that inspires legends; two of the greatest of them are the expeditions of Mallory and Irvine in 1924 and Hillary and Tenzing in 1953. The first of them was a heroic failure, resulting in the deaths of both men; the second was a glorious success, leading to the first climb to the top of Everest. Why was one expedition successful and the other a failure?

FINGER-STICKING GOOD

Explorer David Hempleman-Adams recommends keeping a pencil handy when exploring frozen mountains. If you rub a pencil on a zipper it acts like oil, stopping it from freezing and sticking, and this saves you from having to take off your gloves and losing your fingers to frostbite.

Death on Everest

Mallory and Irvine were last seen when some clouds briefly parted. They were two moving specks not far from the summit.

George Mallory was one of the best mountaineers of his time, and Sandy Irvine was an expert in using oxygen cylinders, the new technology that made it possible to climb into the Death Zone. But several things were against the two men. The cylinders available were heavy and leaky, so they may have run out of oxygen. The weather that year was very bad, and Mallory rushed his attempt to reach the top to try to beat snow that was due to arrive. Most importantly, Mallory and Irvine probably chose the wrong route to the top, which is why most experts believe they never made it.

Top of the world

The 1953 British expedition to Everest was very well organized and prepared. It had a great leader—John Hunt—who made sure everyone did what they needed to. They had the best equipment, including specially developed boots, tents, and oxygen cylinders, and had scientists working out the best way to use their oxygen. They used clever tricks, like bringing builder's ladders to get across crevasses (a trick still used today). Above all they had teamwork, with some members doing lots of hard climbing and carrying, so that Edmund Hillary and Sherpa Tenzing Norgay had the best possible chance to get to the top.

Equipment—1953

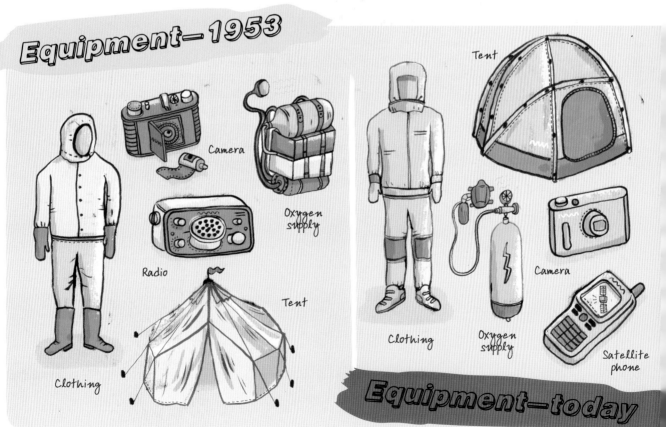

Camera

Oxygen supply

Radio

Tent

Clothing

Tent

Camera

Clothing

Oxygen supply

Satellite phone

Equipment—today

ALIVE!

Mountain explorers go into the mountains with lots of equipment and supplies. What happens to people who end up on a mountain without any of these? Could you survive if you were stranded on a mountain?

THE MIRACLE OF THE ANDES

In 1972, a Uruguayan plane carrying 45 people crashed in the high Andes. Some of the passengers died in the crash and others in an avalanche that hit the crashed plane, but 16 of them survived for 72 days. With no other options, the survivors made the difficult decision to eat the only food available— the frozen bodies of their dead friends and relatives. Eventually, two of the survivors were able to climb several mountains and trek down out of the Andes to get help, using insulation from the airplane they had stitched together into a sleeping bag to survive the freezing nights.

Could you eat your frozen friends if it meant you could live?

TOUCHING THE VOID

In 1985, British climbers Joe Simpson and Simon Yates climbed the West Face of Siula Grande in the Peruvian Andes, a previously unclimbed route. Disaster struck on the way down when Simpson slipped and broke his leg. To get down a cliff Yates had to lower Simpson on a rope, but Simpson ended up stuck in midair, unable to go up or down. Eventually Yates had to cut the rope. Simpson fell into a deep crevasse in a glacier but survived. He knew that Yates would think he was dead, so he had to ignore the pain, rappel down the crevasse, climb up onto the glacier, and hop and crawl back to camp. Without food or water, it took him three days, but somehow he made it.

Would you have the strength to achieve the impossible?

DIY SIGNALING FOR RESCUE

TRY THIS

If you need rescuing you should make rescue symbols on the ground, so that they can be seen from the air. Try this in your back yard.

- Three of anything is the basic international rescue symbol. For instance, arrange three piles of white stones to form a triangle.

- Use light-colored cloth or white stones, or even branches, to make ground-to-air symbols. "V" means "need help;" an "X" means "need medical help."

- Make the symbols at least 6.5 feet (2m) wide and 20 feet (6m) long.

Get ship shape under sail!

What's the right boat for rapids? See page 106.

Where's the treasure?
See page 103.

Don't let a storm sink you! See page 95.

OCEANS & RIVERS

Twisting the cloth tight, you squeeze the last drops of water out of the chopped-up fish bones, and into your mouth. A frigate bird gets caught in one of your traps. Should you rip out its throat with your teeth and drink its blood, or let it go and follow it to the remote island you are searching for, the one inhabited by a tribe who know the location of buried pirate treasure?

Are rafts risky? See page 107!

Under the waves—the last frontier!

EXPLORER'S QUEST

Exploring the watery world is the closest you can get to exploring outer space without leaving Planet Earth. The oceans and seas are completely alien to humans, and even traveling by river can be strange and dangerous. But water is also the explorer's friend—it is much easier to travel great distances by boat than on foot, and only by crossing water can you explore truly unknown lands. Which challenge will you go for?

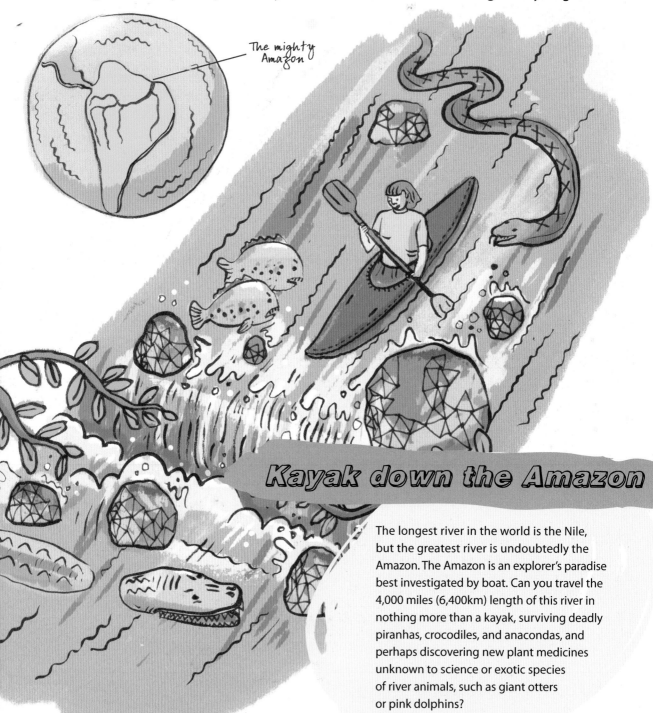

The mighty Amazon

Kayak down the Amazon

The longest river in the world is the Nile, but the greatest river is undoubtedly the Amazon. The Amazon is an explorer's paradise best investigated by boat. Can you travel the 4,000 miles (6,400km) length of this river in nothing more than a kayak, surviving deadly piranhas, crocodiles, and anacondas, and perhaps discovering new plant medicines unknown to science or exotic species of river animals, such as giant otters or pink dolphins?

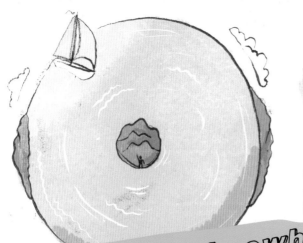

The middle of nowhere

Explorers like to get away from the hustle and bustle, and you can't get any further away than by visiting one of the world's most remote islands. The speck of land that is officially furthest away from any other speck of land is Bouvet Island in the South Atlantic, 1,090 miles (1,750km) off the coast of Antarctica, and 1,400 miles (2,200km) away from the nearest humans. The most remote inhabited island is Tristan de Cunha, in the South Atlantic about halfway between South Africa and South America. Could you sail there and land safely?

Fisherman's fiend

There are some very big fish in the sea, but you don't expect to be eaten while exploring by river. Meet the Mekong giant catfish and think again. This freshwater monster can be up to 9 feet (2.7m) long and weigh nearly 660 pounds (300kg); it is as big as a grizzly bear. Could you catch one while exploring Southeast Asia's mighty Mekong?

TREASURE HUNTERS

Treasure hunting is a specialized branch of exploring, combining the excitement of pirates, shipwrecks, and lost gold with the scientific and historical interest of uncovering old coins and ships of bygone eras. There are more than 3 million shipwrecks in the oceans and seas of the world, and some of these contain so much treasure they are worth over a billion dollars each. To give just one example, a Spanish treasure fleet of eleven ships was lost in 1715 off the coast of Florida. Four of the ships, and the fleet's most valuable treasure, the dowry for the Queen of Spain, have never been found. Can you brave storms, strong currents, and sharks to find the priceless jewels of a lost queen?

VESSELS OF DISCOVERY

Heading off over the horizon without knowing where you are going—or even if there is somewhere to go to—is brave, especially when you may have to deal with terrifying storms, giant waves, sea monsters, and scurvy. You need a vessel to which you can trust your life.

Explorers' boats

If you are a billionaire playboy explorer you might want to equip your luxury super-yacht with a mini submarine, helicopter pad (and helicopter), and a seaplane slingshot launcher. On the other hand, if you are more into classic, solo exploration, you are likely to be interested in one of these three vessels.

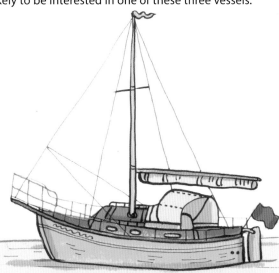

❷ TRANS-OCEANIC ROWBOAT Perhaps you could break the record for the youngest person to row across an ocean? You will need one of these specialized boats, which has an enclosed, water-proof cabin for sleeping and riding out storms, and sliding seats for long hours of rowing.

❸ LIFE RAFT If things don't go well you could find yourself adrift in one of these. Modern life rafts have shelters, special pumps for making drinking water out of seawater, and radio beacons to help rescuers find you. But you will still need to know how to survive on the ocean (see pages 96–97).

❶ YACHT Consider a small sailing yacht with a cosy cabin and equipment that lets you steer and work the sails on your own. This is the sort of boat that single-handed round-the-world sailors use. The modern explorer can take advantage of lots of technology, such as satellite tracking systems so you always know exactly where you are (although this seems like cheating); satellite phones to talk to base; and sonar and radar to help you avoid obstacles and track down shipwrecks.

NEXT STOP THE MOON

TIMELINE OF EXPLORERS' BOATS

The earliest sea explorers were the first humans to leave Africa—many of them probably went by sea to reach places like Arabia, India, Indonesia and Australia. Since those times, sea-going technology has advanced a long way.

Prehistory-modern day: Dugout canoe—hollowed-out logs used to paddle close to shore or to reach offshore islands.

8th century: Currach—a simple boat made from a wooden frame covered with oak or hides, with a single mast. Irish monks may have reached Iceland as early as AD790 using these boats.

800-1200: Outrigger canoe—used by the Polynesians to settle islands spread across thousands of kilometers of empty ocean in the Pacific.

800-1000: Viking longship—a long wooden boat with high pointed ends, equipped with a sail and oars. These had a shallow enough draft to travel rivers but were also capable of crossing wild and stormy oceans.

1405-1433: Junk—Chinese sailing ship. Some versions were enormous, such as the fleet used by China's Ming dynasty explorer Admiral Zheng He, who travelled as far as Africa (see page 101).

1450-1600: Caravel—a small but very tough sailing ship with a round belly, high back end and two lateen (triangular) sails, developed by the Portuguese to explore the coast of Africa and eventually reach Asia and the Americas. These were possibly the greatest ship design in the history of ocean exploration.

1691: Diving bell—a bell-shaped metal vessel for exploring underwater. The basic technology had existed for over 2,000 years, but in 1691, the astronomer Edmund Halley designed one especially for exploring.

1768: Collier—a ship for carrying coal. The sturdy design of the 18th century collier made it the perfect ship for Captain Cook to use for his first voyage of exploration. Renamed the *Endeavour*, Cook's collier went round the world and explored Polynesia, New Zealand and Australia.

1947: Balsa log raft—Norwegian explorer Thor Heyerdahl built a raft called the *Kon-Tiki* out of balsa logs in South America and sailed it to Polynesia (see page 101).

1960: Bathyscape—a deepwater submersible designed to withstand incredible pressure. The bathyscape *Trieste* became the first vessel to reach the deepest point on Earth's surface—the Challenger Deep at the bottom of the Pacific.

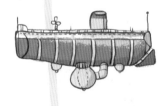

1968: Bermudan ketch—a small two-masted sailing yacht. Robin Knox-Johnston's ketch *Suhaili* was the first boat to be sailed solo, nonstop around the world.

2012: Deep sea submarine—film director James Cameron piloted his specially developed solo submarine *Deepsea Challenger* to the bottom of the Challenger Deep in 2012.

MEET THE LOCALS

· ·

POLYNESIANS

Polynesians are the native inhabitants of the region called
Polynesia, which covers a huge area of the Pacific and includes
islands like Hawaii, New Zealand, and Easter Island. Polynesians
are experts at sailing and navigating so they are able to cross
huge distances at sea without losing their way. Great explorers
themselves, they have many lessons to teach trainee explorers.

CONNECTED BY THE OCEAN

The Polynesians originally came from island
peoples in the west of the Pacific, from around
New Guinea. About 3,000 years ago they reached
the first Polynesian islands to be settled—Tonga
and Samoa. Here they developed their unique
culture, and also the wayfinding techniques that
enabled them to discover new islands thousands of miles away, and travel between them.
Although enormous distances separate these
islands, the Polynesians like to say that the ocean
doesn't keep them apart—it connects them.

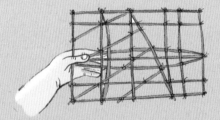

STICK CHART

The Polynesians' neighbors—the
Micronesians—used stick charts to
help navigate the Pacific. The sticks
represented islands, wind directions
and ocean currents.

Knowing how to make
and use stick charts was
"secret business," passed
down from father to son.

WAYFINDING

Wayfinding is the Polynesian art of trans-oceanic navigation; in other words, the special skills and tricks they use to find distant specks of land in a vast ocean, without using compasses, clocks, satellite trackers, or any other technology. Wayfinding skills include:

- Recognizing "seamarks" —these are like watery landmarks. If you know how to look, you can use wave patterns, water color and swell (the way the ocean moves up and down) as seamarks.

- Knowing the stars and constellations and being able to measure how far above the horizon they are.

- Looking at nature—birds, sea life, seaweed, and other natural signposts can tell you how far you are from land and what direction to go.

- Understanding the winds and currents so that you can take advantage of them to push you toward specific islands.

- Observing clouds—islands in the ocean create their own special clouds, and you can see these from much further away than the actual island itself.

AS THE TERN FLIES

Even on a clear day you need to get within 10 miles (16km) of a Pacific island to see it, but birds who live on the island can be seen much further out to sea and followed home. Learn to recognize terns, which travel up to 30 miles (50km) from land, and frigate birds, which travel up to 100 miles (160km).

OCEAN DANGERS

Water is not your natural environment—you can't breathe under it, you can't swim as well as any of the creatures that live in it, and in most parts of the world, you will lose heat so quickly that you will be dead from the cold within a few hours at most.

Holed below the waterline

The greatest threat to your ship is having a hole gashed in it by rocks, reefs, or ice. Use the best charts available to steer clear of rocks and reefs. Don't sail in waters filled with icebergs, and if you have to, remember that they are bigger below the water than above, so give them plenty of space.

SEA SICKNESS

According to old "sea dogs," there are two phases of seasickness:

- **Phase 1:** You feel so sick you think you might die.
- **Phase 2:** You feel so sick you wish you were dead.

Take seasickness pills with you on your expedition.

Battle a shark

Although sharks are terrifying, you are much more likely to be hit by lightning or fall down a manhole than get eaten by a shark. In shark-infested waters, don't go swimming, especially when it gets dark, and don't trail your hands or feet over the edge of the boat. A shark can smell a single drop of blood in an Olympic-size swimming pool, so be particularly careful if you have a cut.

How to fight off a shark attack...

1. Don't splash about or panic. The shark will think you are a wounded fish and is more likely to attack.

NEVER WORK WITH CHILDREN OR ANIMALS THEY TOLD ME...

Storms

Don't be a fair-weather sailor. Learn how to cope with storms, or you will never sail around Cape Horn at the bottom of South America, or even make it through the Bay of Biscay to exotic France. Watch for storm warnings, such as growing swells (heaving of the ocean) and changes in the color of the sky. Reef (roll up) your sails, so they don't get ripped to shreds by the wind, and put out a sea anchor. This will keep your boat facing the oncoming waves, so you won't capsize.

EXPECT THE UNEXPECTED

Danger can come from the most unlikely place. Ask Toby, the pet pig taken to the Antarctic in 1903 by French explorer Jean-Baptiste Charcot. Toby ate a whole bucket of fish without waiting for anyone to take the hooks out of them, and died a painful death.

2 Move slowly toward your boat or the shore.

3 If you're with someone else, get back to back in the water so it can't sneak up on you. If near a rock or reef, back up against it.

4 If a shark attacks you, fight back! Aim for the eyes and gills, the most sensitive spots, with any weapon you can use or make up. Use a fast stabbing motion.

OUCH! YOU BIG MEANY

LOST AT SEA

Disaster! A passing whale has carelessly smashed a hole in your hull. Freezing water crashes into your cabin, waking you to a living nightmare. You have less than a minute to grab what you need and get off your sinking ship, or you will be carried down to Davy Jones' Locker.

Abandon ship

Ocean explorers should always pack a "grab bag"—a large bag containing the essentials for survival. This should include a flashlight, dry clothes, foil blanket, emergency rations, fishing gear, signaling mirror, and flares. In an emergency, activate your inflatable life raft, grab the bag, and go.

life raft

Paddles

Entertainment

Flares

Survival bag

Whistle

Fishing Kit

Canned food

Knife

Locator beacon

Bailing bucket

Water purifier

First aid kit

POON LIM

The British navy teach their sailors about the amazing story of Poon Lim, a Chinese sailor who was working on a British cargo ship during World War Two. When it was torpedoed off the coast of Brazil he survived for 133 days in a life raft by being clever about how to find water and food, and by not giving up.

TRY THIS

DIY—MAKE YOUR OWN COMPASS

You will need a needle, a magnet, a cork, pliers, a thimble, and a bowl of water.

1. Rub the magnet along the needle several times, always in the same direction.

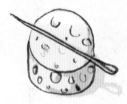

2. Using the pliers and the thimble, push the needle through the middle of the cork, long ways. Warning! This can be difficult and dangerous. Try using a flat piece of cork with a needle-shaped groove across the top, and lay the needle in the groove.

3. Float the cork in a bowl of water on top of a table. It should swing around to line up with north and south. You have made a compass.

SURVIVAL TIPS

- Never drink seawater. It is too salty and will just make you more thirsty, and eventually it will drive you mad and kill you.

- Don't eat unless you have enough to drink. Digesting food uses up water.

- Don't drink on the first day, so that your body goes into water preservation mode.

- Protect your skin from the sun by smearing oil from fish livers onto it. Dry the livers in the sun first.

- Fish eyes, bones, and flesh are sources of water. Eat the eyes and flesh raw and squeeze the bones in a cloth.

- If you are overheating, soak a cloth in seawater and put it round your neck.

- Water that is not good for drinking can still be used—by putting it up your bottom! This is called a rehydration enema.

- Blood from birds and turtles is a good source of water.

DESERT ISLAND SURVIVAL

Robinson Crusoe is a famous character from a book, who was shipwrecked on a island and survived. He was based on a real life survivor, but don't be fooled into thinking that life on a desert island is easy.

Desert island menu

Your priorities are the same as in any survival situation: find shelter, find water, find food, in that order. On a desert island you need to be careful of sunstroke (see page 41), sunburn, and getting soaked by rain storms. If the island is big enough, there should be streams for fresh water, but otherwise look for coconuts, bamboo, vines, and banana trees, which can all be useful sources of drinking water. Don't eat fish from the reef, as they may be poisonous, but do eat crabs, lobsters, sea urchins, sea cucumbers, mussels, barnacles, and sea slugs. Rinse seaweed in freshwater and then boil it.

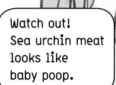

Watch out! Sea urchin meat looks like baby poop.

OPEN A COCONUT

Coconut water is delicious and good for you. If you find a green coconut cut off the top. A hard, brown one is more difficult to break into. Stick a thick branch into the ground and sharpen the end to a point. Use it to split the hairy outer husk and then to make a hole in the top of the shell.

Don't drink too much coconut water or you will get terrible diarrhea.

Message in a bottle

Your best hope of rescue is by building a triangle of signal fires, or using a mirror to signal to passing aircraft, but you could try putting a message in a bottle and throwing it in the sea. Just don't expect an answer anytime soon. Although glass is resistant to seawater, the cork could come loose or rot, and the bottle could get smashed on rocks if it ever comes ashore. If it catches the right current it could end up almost anywhere. One message in a bottle took 92 years (from 1914 to 2006) to travel from the middle of the North Sea to the Shetland Islands—hopefully it wasn't from someone asking to be rescued.

ALEXANDER SELKIRK

Robinson Crusoe was based on real-life Scottish sailor, Alexander Selkirk. He was working on a pirate ship in 1704, but he was so sure that the poorly captained ship would sink that he demanded to be abandoned on a tiny uninhabited island called Más a Tierra (now known as Robinson Crusoe Island), 420 miles (675km) off the coast of Chile. He sat down and read his Bible, waiting to be rescued, but soon realized that no one was coming. Over four years later Selkirk was picked up by a passing ship. They discovered a "wildman" dressed in goat skins. Being left behind had saved Selkirk's life because his original ship had indeed sunk and its crew were either drowned or rotting in jail.

Selkirk made friends with some wild cats. They kept rats from attacking him at night.

TO BOLDLY GO...

The greatest names in exploration are ocean-going explorers who made incredible voyages of discovery. They were brave men because setting off in a sailing ship across the ocean, when no one knew what was on the other side, was the equivalent of going into space at the time.

CALAMITY COLUMBUS

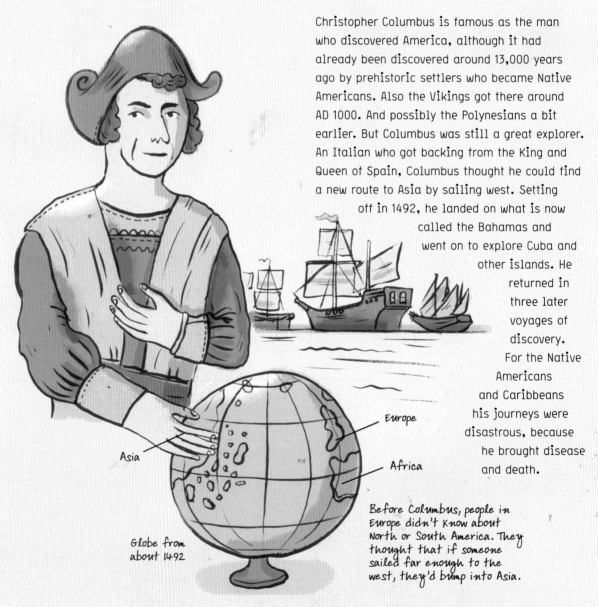

Christopher Columbus is famous as the man who discovered America, although it had already been discovered around 13,000 years ago by prehistoric settlers who became Native Americans. Also the Vikings got there around AD 1000. And possibly the Polynesians a bit earlier. But Columbus was still a great explorer. An Italian who got backing from the King and Queen of Spain, Columbus thought he could find a new route to Asia by sailing west. Setting off in 1492, he landed on what is now called the Bahamas and went on to explore Cuba and other islands. He returned in three later voyages of discovery. For the Native Americans and Caribbeans his journeys were disastrous, because he brought disease and death.

Europe

Asia

Africa

Globe from about 1492

Before Columbus, people in Europe didn't know about North or South America. They thought that if someone sailed far enough to the west, they'd bump into Asia.

A LOAD OF JUNK

Zheng He is possibly the greatest explorer no one has ever heard of. He was prime minister of the Ming dynasty empire of China, and was put in charge of a series of massive expeditions of discovery, trade, and tribute between 1405 and 1433, which traveled through Southeast Asia to India and Africa. He sailed in fleets of junks, Chinese sailing ships; on his fourth voyage he had 63 huge ships, some of which were 260 feet (80m) long.

THESE JUNKS AINT JUNK!

By using the most up-to-date technology and the best equipment, Zheng He gave himself the greatest chance of success.

THE KON-TIKI EXPEDITION

In 1947, Norwegian explorer Thor Heyerdahl set out to prove that Polynesia could have been settled by explorers from South America, after hearing legends about a mythological god called Tiki who came to Polynesia from the East. In Peru he built a 45-foot (14-m) long raft out of nine balsa tree trunks, with a cabin and a mast for sails; he called it *Kon-Tiki*, after an old name for the Inca sun god. Heyerdahl and his crewmates sailed and drifted nearly 4,000 miles (6,500km) until they reached some islands near Tahiti.

Balsa wood is very light and strong.

UNDER THE SEA

Technology has made it possible for ocean explorers to go beneath the waves; at first for very short periods and only to shallow depths, but now for long periods to the very bottom of the ocean. The ocean deeps are the last great frontier for exploration on Earth. It is often said that we know more about the surface of the Moon than the bottom of the sea, yet the oceans cover more than 70 percent of our planet.

Going down

If you want to explore underwater you have a number of options, depending how deep you want to go.

SNORKELING
This lets you swim at the surface, looking down while breathing through a tube called a snorkel. Put some fins on your feet and you can move along quite fast.

SCUBA DIVING
Scuba (Self-Contained Underwater Breathing Apparatus) diving uses tanks of compressed air to allow people to breathe underwater. This is the closest you can get to being a fish.

DIVING BELLS
These work by simple physics. If you turn a bucket over in the bath and push it down, the air inside is trapped. The water pressure may squash it very slightly but it won't disappear. If you were inside, you could breathe the air and look at the bottom of the bath. A diving bell works on the same principle. Hoses supply fresh air to replace the air you've used up, and you can look out of the bottom of the bell at the seabed.

DIVING SUIT
These function in a similar way as a diving bell—it is basically a diving bell that covers your head, leaving your legs free to walk around on the bottom.

SUBMARINES
Vehicles that can move about underwater are called submarines. The most advanced exploration submarine is probably film director James Cameron's *Deepsea Challenger*, which in 2012 descended 6.8 miles (11km) to the lowest point on Earth's surface.

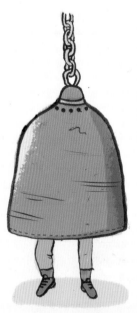

Under pressure

Freediving is simply swimming underwater while holding your breath. If you know how to equalize the pressure of the air inside your ears with the water pushing into them, there is no limit to how deep you can go, except for how long you can hold your breath. The record is 702 feet (214m), but be warned, freediving is very dangerous. Never, ever dive without a dive buddy (someone to keep an eye on you).

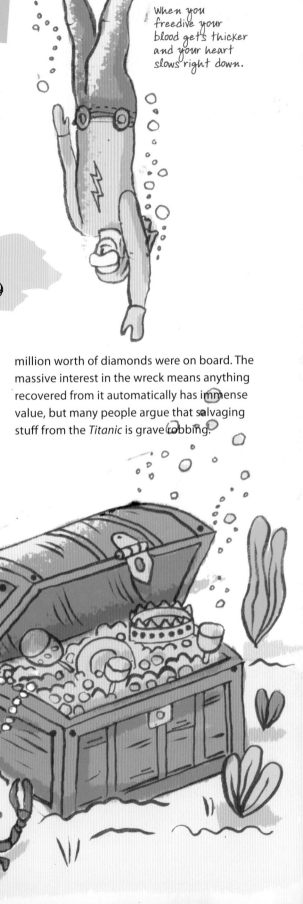

When you freedive your blood gets thicker and your heart slows right down.

Greatest sunken treasures of all time

Three of the most valuable sunken treasure shipwrecks of all time are...

- The S.S. *Republic*: A United States Civil War-era steamship loaded with gold and silver that sunk off the coast of Georgia in 1865. It was found in 2003. Salvors have recovered about a quarter of its estimated $300 million worth of coins.

- *Nuestra Senora de Atocha*: The richest wreck ever salvaged, the *Atocha* was a Spanish treasure galleon that sank off the Florida Keys in 1622. Treasure hunter Mel Fisher found it in 1985 and over $450 million of treasure has since been recovered.

- *Titanic*: The most famous shipwreck in the world sank in 1912 in the North Atlantic after hitting an iceberg. Passengers included dozens of the world's richest people, who would have carried many of their jewels with them, and one treasure hunter believes that $300 million worth of diamonds were on board. The massive interest in the wreck means anything recovered from it automatically has immense value, but many people argue that salvaging stuff from the *Titanic* is grave robbing.

RIVER DANGERS

What do you think of when you imagine canoeing down a river? Probably clear water running slowly and smoothly between grassy banks, while you paddle lazily along. Wrong! Think again. Rivers can be murky, violent places, hiding deadly dangers that want to kill you (it's probably not personal).

Whirlpool

Whirlpools are circular currents spiraling down into the water. They are formed where streams collide, or where the water is blocked by things like big rocks or sharp bends. If the whirlpool is big and strong enough it can suck down a whole boat—and you with it. This could be deadly news for an open canoe, which will fill with water and sink, but if you're in a kayak you should be fine because most whirlpools die out quickly as they move along the river, allowing you to bob up to the surface. Either way, the best way to handle a whirlpool is to avoid it or, if you can get a good look at it, work out on which side the current is going downstream. Paddle into that part and you can get an acceleration boost that will slingshot you out the other side.

Crude catfish

Perhaps the most terrifying danger in the world for explorers is the candiru, a tiny catfish with a horrible habit. It lives in the Amazon where it burrows into the gills of bigger fish and uses its spines to stick there while feeding off their blood. It can squirm into all sorts of narrow passages, including the urethra—that's the tube that you pee out of! Once in there, it will burrow into your flesh to drink your blood. Explorers should stay covered up while in the Amazon, and keep a safe distance from the water while urinating.

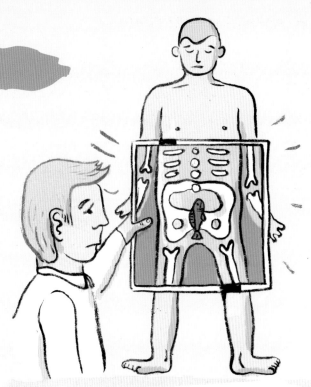

Electric eels

I'VE GOT A SHOCKING HEADACHE

Lurking in muddy pools around the rivers of South America are huge fish with amazing super-powers. Known as electric eels, they are actually relatives of the catfish. They can grow to 8 feet (2.5m) long (about twice the height of an eight-year old boy). These eels have hundreds of tiny natural batteries in their bodies, and they can give an electric shock five times stronger than you would get from sticking your fingers in a plug at home—powerful enough to knock a horse off its feet.

Bull sharks

This shark species survives happily in the open ocean, and hundreds of miles up rivers. Because of their wide distribution and aggression, many experts consider them the most dangerous sharks in the world.

TYPES OF RIVER BOATS AND RAFTS

Your boat is not just for carrying you up or down river—it is also your pack mule, porter, shelter, safety capsule, and, probably, heaviest piece of gear. So you need to make sure you choose the right vessel for your needs; balancing weight, speed, how easy it is to handle, how much it can carry, and, crucially, how many people it can carry. Hardcore explorers don't believe in cheats like motors or engines, so for a small expedition, you have three main choices of self-powered river craft: canoe, kayak, or raft.

WE'RE UP A CREEK WITH A PADDLE!

Canoe

Based on old Native American boats, canoes are small, narrow, open boats, with seats for two or more people, each using a paddle with a single blade (although you can also use oars, sails, or poles). Canoes are the first choice for most river explorers: good for carrying people and supplies, they can even be carried from one watercourse to another.

Kayak

Modeled on old Inuit boats, kayaks look a bit like small canoes, except they usually have covered decks. There are one or two cockpits, depending how many pilots the kayak has, and each of these is fitted with a spray "skirt" (cover), so that when the pilot is seated there are no gaps to allow water to get into the boat. Kayak pilots use a paddle with a blade at each end. Kayaks are best for explorers who want to go off on their own, or expect to go over rapids where a river flows over rocks and down steep slopes.

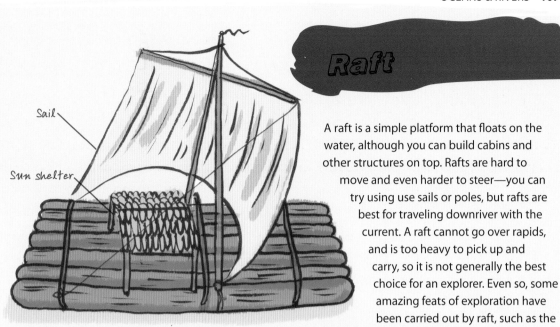

Sail

Sun shelter

Raft

A raft is a simple platform that floats on the water, although you can build cabins and other structures on top. Rafts are hard to move and even harder to steer—you can try using use sails or poles, but rafts are best for traveling downriver with the current. A raft cannot go over rapids, and is too heavy to pick up and carry, so it is not generally the best choice for an explorer. Even so, some amazing feats of exploration have been carried out by raft, such as the voyage of the *Kon-Tiki* (see page 101).

LEWIS AND CLARK'S IRONBOAT

Perhaps the greatest river exploration expedition in history was the Lewis and Clark Expedition of 1804-06, in which a small party of explorers known as the Corps of Discovery traveled up the Missouri and down the Columbia rivers to reach the Pacific. The Corps used 25 boats of five different types during their epic journey, including an unusual contraption called the *Ironboat*. It had a collapsible iron frame so that it could be carried around and set up when needed.

The Ironboat's whereabouts are unknown, so perhaps a modern-day explorer could find it, probably somewhere in Montana.

ROLLING ON THE RIVER

The river explorer's greatest foes are not crocodiles or piranhas, although these are pretty nasty, but rapids and waterfalls. You could try to canoe or kayak over these, in which case you have to be prepared for your boat to capsize (see opposite); or you could go around them by land, in which case you need to know how to pick up your boat.

Portage

Sometimes you will have to pick up your boat and carry it around an obstacle or to another river on foot—this is called portage. Even though river boats are designed to weigh as little as possible for their size, they are still heavy. In fact portage can be the most difficult and tiring part of river exploration.

Kayaks are light, and should be easy to carry, like a suitcase or hoist onto your shoulder, but picking up a canoe is a special skill that you will need to practice.

1 Face the canoe and grab the near gunwale (rim) in the middle. Lift the side of the canoe and take a step forward.

2 Lean into the boat and grab the center of the bar across the middle—this is called the carrying yoke, and is there specially to help you lift the boat. Keep your back straight and lean backward, bending your knees so that the canoe lifts onto your thighs.

3 Move your forward hand along the yoke bar to grip the far gunwale, and move your other hand along the bar toward you until it reaches the near gunwale. Keep the canoe balanced on your thighs.

4 Smoothly roll and swing the canoe onto your head.

5 Lower the canoe onto your shoulders so that the yoke bar sits across them. You are now ready to portage your canoe.

Screw roll

Before you set off exploring in your kayak, make sure you know how to roll out of a capsize. One technique is the screw roll.

1 If you roll over, wait until upside down, then twist your body, lean forward, reach up, and put your paddle out of the water.

2 Roll your right wrist to make sure the right paddle blade is facing the water. Bring it down into the water in a sweep away from the front of the kayak toward the back.

3 The kayak will start to twist. Untwist your body so that you face forward, while still sweeping the paddle back.

4 When the paddle is pointing straight down, snap up your right hip.

5 Keep your head and body in the water until the last moment. When the boat rolls level they will come out of the water.

If all else fails and you are still underwater, release your spray skirt, put your hands on the rim of the cockpit, and push the kayak up and forward to get your legs clear so you can float free.

GETTING THEIR FEET WET

Many great explorers traveled by river for some or all of their voyages of exploration. Rivers are brilliant ways to cover large distances while carrying plenty of equipment and food, but most importantly they will almost always lead you to safety, because if you follow them downstream far enough you will eventually find other people.

DOWN THE MISSISSIPPI

The first Europeans to thoroughly explore the mighty Mississippi were Louis Jolliet, a fur trader from Quebec, and Father Jacques Marquette, a French priest. Jolliet was perhaps the greatest river explorer in North American history, having already explored the Great Lakes and many other rivers in America. In 1673 he and Marquette traveled most of the length of the Mississippi, but he lost all his notes and the maps he had made while going over some rapids. Fortunately Jolliet had a great memory, and was able to write them down again.

DIY DRY BAG

The simplest way to make a dry bag is to use a plastic bag with no holes (e.g. a large freezer bag).

1 Put your stuff (e.g. maps, pictures) inside the bag, and squeeze out the air.

2 Roll up the top, from one side to the other.

3 Twist the rolled up section.

4 Fold it over and put a tight rubber band around the fold.

Test it out by putting it underwater in a sink or bath.

MADDENING MOSQUITOES

Mina Hubbard's husband, Leonidas, died while exploring the rivers of Labrador, eastern Canada in 1903. She decided to finish what he had started, so in 1905 she set off down the North West River with the help of four guides. Although they braved fierce rapids, Hubbard's biggest problems were the swarms of mosquitoes and flies that constantly tried to eat her. She wore home-made masks with netting covering her face, but she could feel the blood running down her neck from all the bites!

> Mosquitoes, midges, and biting flies are a serious problem for all river explorers. Bring plenty of repellent, and pack mosquito nets and other protective gear.

THE AMAZON BY ACCIDENT

One of the great voyages of river exploration was made by accident in 1538. Spaniard Francisco de Orellana was part of an expedition looking for El Dorado, the fabled city of gold in South America (see page 17). He and his men became separated from the rest of the expedition and decided to build some boats, as he was sure that El Dorado was just around the bend. Eventually he followed the river all the way to the sea, traveling almost the entire length of the Amazon. He returned to South America in 1546, but the expedition was a disaster and he died.

> It is much, much easier to travel down a river than up it.

Airship—blast from the past or the shape of things to come?

AIR

Your map says that directly underneath you there should be a tiny island complete with tiny runway—the last stop in your record-breaking round-the-world flight—but in reality there is only endless blue ocean. You check the fuel gauge: there's only a few minutes until you run out. Should you turn back and head for the last land you flew over, or continue zig-zagging along your current bearing, and hope you reach the island for which you were aiming?

What keeps airplanes in the air? Lift! What's lift? See page 120.

Hot air balloon—go where the breeze takes you.

EXPLORER'S QUEST

Aviation (flying machine) technology was an important breakthrough for explorers. Not only did it make it possible to travel great distances quickly and visit places previously impossible to reach, it also opened a new frontier for exploration and achievement. Today's aerial explorers still push back these frontiers, as well as revisiting the early flights of yesteryear.

FIND EARHART

Perhaps the most famous name in the history of aerial exploration is Amelia Earhart. She was a pioneering female pilot (or aviatrix) who became a global celebrity after flying solo across the Atlantic (the first woman to do so). In 1937, she and her navigator Fred Noonan disappeared over the Pacific while attempting a record-breaking round-the-world flight. One of the largest search operations in history found no trace of her, but intriguing clues suggest she may have survived for a short time on a tiny desert island (see page 119). Could you retrace her final steps, and solve one of the greatest mysteries in aviation history?

Pole to pole

Flying around the world (aerial circumnavigation) has been done many times in many different ways (for instance, in 2005, billionaire adventurer, Steve Fossett flew around the world non-stop without refueling). Much less common is aerial polar circumnavigation, which is where you fly around the world from Pole to Pole (rather than following the Equator). The current record is 52½ hours but surely you could do better?

The edge of space

The Karman line, 60 miles (100km) above Earth's surface, is where the atmosphere meets outer space. It is impossible to fly an airplane any higher than this because the atmosphere is too thin, but reaching the Karman line in an airplane is one of the great challenges in aviation. There is also a great deal of important scientific research to be done in this part of the atmosphere, so if you can reach the edge of space you could be a scientific explorer too.

Land on a lost world

A tepui is a flat-topped mountain rising up out of the jungle in South America. The tops of these mountains are cut off from the rest of the world so they form "lost worlds," with unique plants and animals and undisturbed jungles; some people believe dinosaurs might still survive on top of an unexplored tepui. Jimmie Angel was a daredevil pilot who discovered the world's tallest waterfall (now called Angel Falls, 3,212 feet [979m] high) cascading off a tepui called Auyántepui. In 1937 he landed his plane on top of it but the wheels got stuck in the mud so he had to walk back down. Could you copy his daring stunt and land on a tepui?

TO THE SKIES

Explorers can use aircraft in two different ways. One is to explore the skies and push back the frontiers of aviation. The other is to make other types of exploring possible or easier—such as using a helicopter to get to the top of a mountain, or flying across an ocean to reach a distant land.

Airplanes

Airplanes are fast, sturdy, and safe, but they usually need a long flat space for landing and taking off. For instance, when Charles Lindbergh became the first man to fly across the Atlantic in 1927, the most dangerous part of the voyage was the take off. His plane was heavy with fuel and he only just managed to climb above the telephone wires at the end of the runway. One way round the landing strip problem is to use a seaplane—a plane that can land and take off from the sea—or a plane equipped with skis to land on snow or ice.

BUSH PLANE

The ideal plane for an explorer is the bush airplane, a small, propeller-driven light aircraft with high wings (so you can see the ground), high front wheels (to keep the propeller off the ground), and landing gear that can be easily fitted with floats or skis.

Balloons

Balloons were the first aircraft to be invented. The first balloon-crossing of the English Channel was in 1785, 124 years before Louis Bleriot crossed it in an aircraft in 1909. These balloon pioneers were true explorers—no human had ever gone where they went, and nobody knew if it were even possible to survive that high in the sky. Balloons are difficult to steer, are at the mercy of the wind, and they can be extremely dangerous to land. But they are a great choice if you are trying to reach the edge of space.

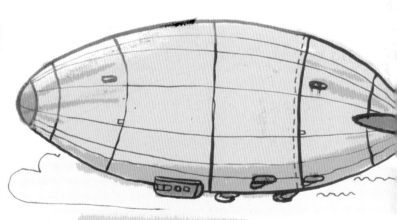

Helicopters

Helicopters don't need runways which makes them ideal for exploring. On the other hand they are very expensive to buy and to run, and they are also not as safe as airplanes when it comes to high winds and poor weather. Some explorers think that using a helicopter is cheating, but if you want to get into a volcano or on top of a tepui, you may not have much choice.

The first ever balloon passengers were a sheep, a duck, and a rooster. They went for an eight-minute sightseeing trip in 1783.

Dirigible

A dirigible (that's French for "steerable") is a balloon-type aircraft that can be steered and powered using propellers or other devices. They are also known as airships, zeppelins, or blimps. They use a lighter-than-air gas (normally helium, which won't catch fire), trapped in a rigid bag. Airships have been used in exploration since the early 20th century, when the airship *Norge*, piloted by Umberto Nobile and with Roald Amundsen on board, in 1926 became the first aircraft to have definitely flown over the North Pole (see page 125).

WHAT GOES UP...

Landing is the most difficult task for an airborne explorer, because where you're going, they don't have runways. Chances are the reason you're exploring by aircraft is exactly because you're headed somewhere hard to reach, and that usually means hard to land on. What are the top three worst places to land?

1. In a volcano

A volcano has steep sides covered with huge, jagged rocks, or thick jungle—or both; clouds of smoke, ash, and steam, as well as poisonous gases you can't see; sudden gusts of wind; and lakes of molten lava that may explode and throw deadly lava bombs into the air. Only a helicopter is suitable for a volcano, and your best bet is to find a part of the crater rim that is relatively flat. In 1992, helicopter pilot, Craig Hosking was flying two cameramen over Hawaii's Kilauea Volcano, where a pool of lava bubbles at the bottom of a 120-foot (35-m) deep pit. Suddenly, gas from the volcano caused his engine to stop working. He realized that his only hope was to land inside the volcano near the bottom of the crater where there was a flat space.

Amazingly, all three of the men survived the crash-landing and were rescued by another helicopter.

2. On a coral reef

Coral polyps grow just below the surface of the sea, building homes out of rock they create themselves. Over time this rock builds up to form a reef, which may be mostly flat but will also be uneven with jagged, spiky bits and deep holes. Normally, a coral reef is the last place you would want to land a plane, but some people believe that Amelia Earhart did just that when she went missing in 1937. Some evidence suggests that she and her navigator, Fred Noonan, made it to a tiny uninhabited coral island called Nikumororo (or Gardner Island). With no fuel left, Earhart would have had no choice but to attempt to land on the reef while it was exposed at low tide. There is no sign of the plane, which could have been washed away by the tide, and if Earhart and Noonan really did make it to the island, they could not have survived there for very long.

3. Lukla Airport

There are about 44,000 airports in the world. Most are carefully planned for easy landings; some, however, can be a little tricky and are for experienced pilots only. Then there is Lukla Airport in Nepal—the scariest airport in the world. Its sloping runway is very short and narrow (1,500 feet x 65 feet or 460m x 20m). It is high up—9,383 feet (2,860m)—which means the air is thin, and airplanes are difficult to control at low speeds. This is a problem because you have to make a sharp turn just before lining up with the runway. Worst of all, at the end of the runway is a stone wall and the side of a steep mountain. Once you are coming in to land you can't change your mind and there will be no second chance. Still, if you're feeling lucky, Lukla is a great place to start your exploration of the Himalayan wilderness around Mount Everest.

AFRAID OF HEIGHTS

The airlines like to boast that traveling on a commercial airliner is safer than driving in a car, but explorers tend to use smaller, riskier aircraft, and visit dangerous places. Exploring by air brings special risks which you need to take into consideration when flying to a remote island, snowy wilderness, or "lost world" on top of a mountain.

Ice

For a small aircraft like a bush plane, ice is one of the greatest dangers. Ice can build up very quickly on an aircraft, even if you took off from somewhere hot, because as you go up through the atmosphere the air gets colder very quickly. Ice can choke your engine, but the biggest danger is that ice on the wing interferes with the flow of air that produces lift (see "Flying 101"), and the aircraft becomes impossible to fly.

FLYING 101

Why doesn't a plane fall out of the sky? The answer is lift. A plane's wings are shaped so that the air rushing past gets pushed downward behind the wing. For every action there is an equal and opposite reaction, so while the air gets pushed down, the wing—and the airplane—gets pushed up. This upward force is called lift, and if you have a big enough wing and are going fast enough, you can make enough lift to fly.

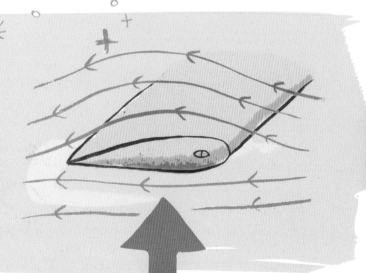

Lost in space

On the ground you always know which way is down, because you have the ground under your feet. But in the air it is easy to get disorientated in all three dimensions. This is a special problem at night; over water, sand, ice, or snow where everything below you looks the same; in heavy clouds or fog where you can't see anything; or when light conditions are confusing, such as at sunset or sunrise. This is where you have to know how to use your instruments to help you—for instance, your compass and your artificial horizon (the dial that shows the angle of the plane relative to the horizon).

Storms

Storms produce high winds, powerful lightning and big hailstones, all of which can damage or cause an aircraft to crash. Most modern aircraft are built so that lightning travels through the outer skin of the airplane without affecting what's inside (which includes you). But there are no magic solutions to high winds, sudden drops in pressure or hailstones. Aviation explorers need to check weather forecasts to decide whether and where to fly, and use their radar and their eyes to fly around storms, not through them. This is much harder in a balloon or airship, which is why they are not popular with modern explorers.

Bird strike

If you hit anything while you are traveling at hundreds of kilometres an hour it generally means trouble. Fortunately the skies are mostly empty, except for those pesky birds. Hitting a bird can destroy a propeller or jet engine and smash parts of the aircraft. Avoid bird strike by not taking off or flying near flocks of birds or places where birds are common, by flying high (most bird strikes happen below 500 feet (150m), although a Griffon vulture once ran into a plane at 37,000 feet [11,300m] over Africa), and by cutting your speed so if you do hit one it's less deadly.

HOW TO LAND A PLANE IN AN EMERGENCY

You are enjoying a well-earned rest in the passenger seat of a bush plane after a hard week's exploring in the jungle, when suddenly your pilot says, "Aaaarrgghh!" Bad luck: a poisonous spider boarded at the same time as you, and now it looks like you will have to learn how to fly a plane very quickly.

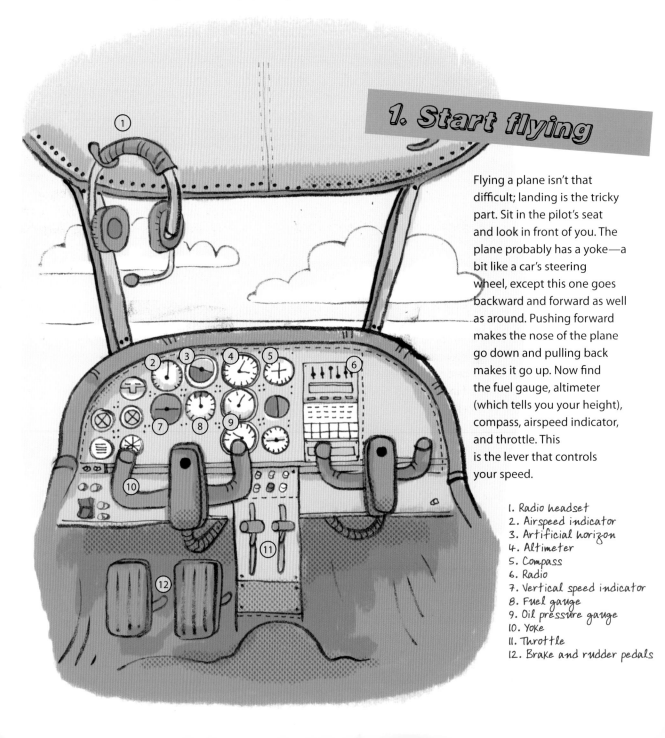

1. Start flying

Flying a plane isn't that difficult; landing is the tricky part. Sit in the pilot's seat and look in front of you. The plane probably has a yoke—a bit like a car's steering wheel, except this one goes backward and forward as well as around. Pushing forward makes the nose of the plane go down and pulling back makes it go up. Now find the fuel gauge, altimeter (which tells you your height), compass, airspeed indicator, and throttle. This is the lever that controls your speed.

1. Radio headset
2. Airspeed indicator
3. Artificial horizon
4. Altimeter
5. Compass
6. Radio
7. Vertical speed indicator
8. Fuel gauge
9. Oil pressure gauge
10. Yoke
11. Throttle
12. Brake and rudder pedals

2. Call for help

Find the radio. Don't change the channel—it is probably already set so that you can speak to someone helpful. Push the talk button and explain your predicament. If no one answers, try frequency 121.5—this is the emergency frequency.

3. Look for a landing place

If you are low on fuel or there is no one to help you, look for a place to land. You need the biggest open space available. If you have to change direction to find one, do it very carefully, pushing the yoke very gently to the side.

4. Cut your speed

Once you are lined up with a landing place, pull back on the throttle until your airspeed indicator shows 90 knots. Keep the nose of the plane just below the horizon. Lower your landing gear if it's not already down. When you get close to the landing field cut the power even more to just over 70 knots, with the nose of the plane just a little below the horizon. Aim to be about 100 feet (30m) off the ground as you reach the edge of the landing site.

5. Brake!

As you reach the ground pull right back on the throttle and at the last moment pull up your nose a bit. Once your wheels hit the ground start using the pedals that work the brake flaps, and if necessary brace yourself for a crash.

6. Breathe out

Congratulations! You just landed a plane. Now catch that poisonous spider, and get your pilot to a hospital.

COLD AIR

By the time airplanes started flying, most of the world had been explored. But this exciting new invention arrived just in time for the race to the Poles—the competition to see who would be the first to reach the North and South Poles.

True north

Surprisingly the South Pole was easier to reach than the North, and Amundsen got there by foot and dog sled in 1911 (see page 61). But traveling on foot to the North Pole turned out to be very difficult, and although the American Arctic explorer Robert Peary claimed to have got there in 1908–1909, a lot of people didn't believe him. Reaching the Pole by air would be the next great adventure in exploration history.

AIRSHIP ADVENTURERS

Just five days after Richard Byrd's polar flight (see page 125), the airship *Norge* took off from Spitsbergen, flew over the North Pole and landed in Alaska. It was the first time anyone had flown right across the Arctic. On board were the pilot, Italian airship designer and pioneer Umberto Nobile, American adventurer Lincoln Ellsworth, and the great Norwegian, Roald Amundsen. Amundsen became the first person to visit both Poles, and today people think he reached both of them first.

CAN YOU PUT A FLAG ON THE NORTH POLE?

There is no land on the North Pole—only ice on top of the Arctic Ocean. This ice is always moving, so if you plant a flag at the North Pole it will soon travel somewhere else. Thanks to global warming the North Pole may become ice free most summers.

LIKE A BYRD

Richard Byrd was a pioneering aviator who was fascinated with the Arctic. In 1925, he launched an expedition to fly over the North Pole, and on May 9th, 1926 he claimed to have done just that in his plane *Josephine Ford*. At the time many people didn't believe Byrd, and it is still thought that his claims were not true.

If you want to claim to be the first to have visited somewhere, you have to prove it. Take pictures and write down dates and details of your position using your map, compass, and GPS.

THE ITALIA DISASTER

Nobile was upset that Amundsen got the credit for their *Norge* expedition, so, in 1928, he tried again with the airship *Italia*. Nobile reached the North Pole but on the way back too much ice built up on the airship and it crashed onto an ice floe, ripping the cabin apart and dumping Nobile and eight others onto the ice. The *Italia* then drifted off with six men still on board who were never seen again. An international rescue effort was launched. Amundsen flew his own plane north to join in, but tragically he crashed and died on the way. Nobile was eventually rescued.

Umberto Nobile's dog Titina could not only claim to have visited the Arctic twice, but also to have peed on the floor of the Oval Office.

NAVIGATION

Which way is the Moon pointing? See page 139.

It's dark and you are lost. If only you hadn't shredded your map when you were trying to fold it, and then lost your compass crossing that river! Luckily it's a clear night, with a crescent moon and a good view of the stars—you should have no trouble working out which way is north. The only question is, should you head off in the dark, or wait until morning and find a hill so you can get a good look around you?

What are all those wiggly lines? See page 129.

Be sure to take your compass. See pages 132–134.

MAP READING

Exploring isn't just about having adventures, fighting off sharks, and rappelling into volcanoes (although these are the best bits). Explorers like to visit places where few, if any, people have ever been, but to get there they need to be able to navigate (find their way) using a map, compass and, sometimes, the Sun, Moon, and stars.

The joy of maps

In the old days the explorer started off with a big blank sheet of paper decorated with some drawings of sea monsters, and it was his or her job to fill it in and make a map. Today there aren't many blank spots left on the map, and as a result, your map is probably your most valuable piece of equipment (after your boots—see page 142). Before you head off into the wilderness, make sure you know how to use your map. You need to know how to read and fold your map, and how to use it with a compass.

A person who makes maps is called a cartographer.

Folding a map

This sounds like a simple task but actually it's all too easy to get wrong. Maps are usually big, with lots of folds, so if you do muck it up you will end up with a big bundle of paper that won't fit in your map case, and the map will tear at the folds and fall apart.

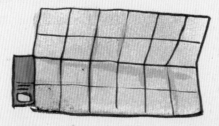

❶ Open up your map until it is fully spread open.

❷ Check the creases and folds. If they are fresh, they will indicate where to fold.

Sticky situations

Lines of longitude

Lines of latitude

If you look at your map you will notice two sorts of lines (not counting roads, rivers, railroads, etc). The straight lines that form a grid on your map are lines of longitude and latitude. These are imaginary lines which map-makers and explorers use as reference points when describing where they are. Lines of longitude run from pole to pole, and they show where you are from east to west. Lines of latitude circle around Earth parallel to the Equator, and they show where you are from north to south.

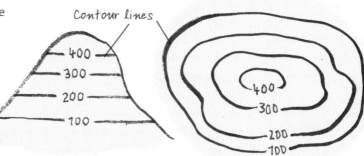

Contour lines

400
300
200
100

400
300
200
100

The other sort of lines on your map are contour lines. A contour line on the map joins up places that are the same height, and they are used to represent hills, mountains, cliffs and valleys on a flat piece of paper. Contour lines close together mean a steep hill while ones that are spread apart indicate a gentle slope. This is important when planning your route.

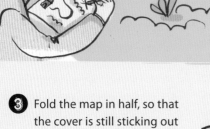

DIY—MAKE A MAP
TRY THIS

A map doesn't have to be covered in contours and symbols, but it should show where things are compared to each other. Explorers should be good at making maps, so practice by drawing a map of your house and garden, or maybe your street and neighborhood. Start off by drawing a grid, and try to keep the same scale throughout the map.

3 Fold the map in half, so that the cover is still sticking out of the side.

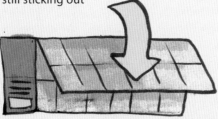

5 Fold over the cover so that it is on the outside.

4 Squeeze the map together like an accordion, but make sure the cover stays on top.

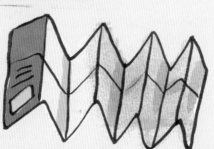

TRUE NORTH

North doesn't just mean "up" on your map. If you understand what north and south mean, and how to find them, you will never get truly lost.

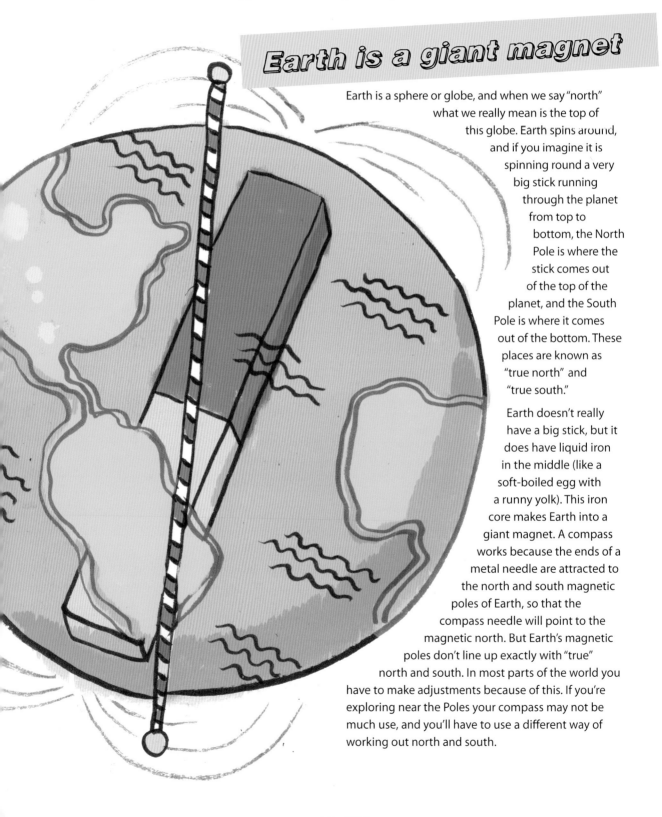

Earth is a giant magnet

Earth is a sphere or globe, and when we say "north" what we really mean is the top of this globe. Earth spins around, and if you imagine it is spinning round a very big stick running through the planet from top to bottom, the North Pole is where the stick comes out of the top of the planet, and the South Pole is where it comes out of the bottom. These places are known as "true north" and "true south."

Earth doesn't really have a big stick, but it does have liquid iron in the middle (like a soft-boiled egg with a runny yolk). This iron core makes Earth into a giant magnet. A compass works because the ends of a metal needle are attracted to the north and south magnetic poles of Earth, so that the compass needle will point to the magnetic north. But Earth's magnetic poles don't line up exactly with "true" north and south. In most parts of the world you have to make adjustments because of this. If you're exploring near the Poles your compass may not be much use, and you'll have to use a different way of working out north and south.

Finding north

There are lots of ways you can find north without a compass—probably the simplest use the movement of the Sun and Moon across the sky. Try out these methods in your back yard.

1 **Sun stick** Put a straight stick upright in the ground in a flat place. Mark the tip of its shadow with a rock. Wait 15 minutes, and then mark the shadow's tip again. Stand with your left foot at the first marker and your right foot at the second marker. You are now facing north. You can do the same thing at night if the Moon is bright enough.

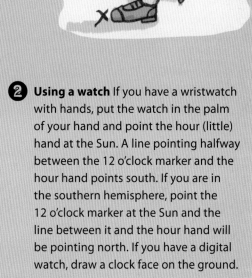

First mark

Second mark

North!

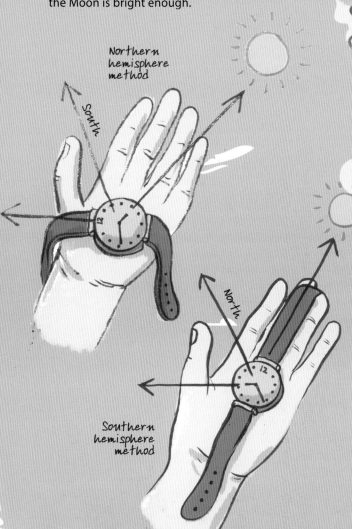

Northern hemisphere method

South

North

Southern hemisphere method

2 **Using a watch** If you have a wristwatch with hands, put the watch in the palm of your hand and point the hour (little) hand at the Sun. A line pointing halfway between the 12 o'clock marker and the hour hand points south. If you are in the southern hemisphere, point the 12 o'clock marker at the Sun and the line between it and the hour hand will be pointing north. If you have a digital watch, draw a clock face on the ground.

COMPASS 101

A compass has a needle that points toward the magnetic north pole. Compasses come in many different shapes and sizes, from tiny button ones (you might want to keep one of these in your emergency pack) to complicated electronic ones. The most common one for explorers is an orienteering compass.

Orienteering with a compass

An orienteering compass is made to use with a map. It is fixed into a see-through plastic card with lines on it, and has a dial you can turn, with an arrow. You can use these to make sure your map is the right way around, to decide which direction to go in, and to make sure you keep going in the right direction.

For instance, to orient your map (i.e. make sure it is lined up with north)...

1 Line up the sides of the compass with the north-south lines on your map.

2 Turn the big arrow until is pointing to map north.

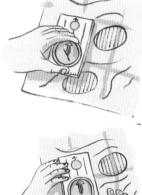

3 Hold the map and compass together as you turn round, until the red end of the compass needle lines up with the big arrow.

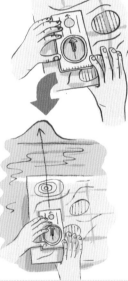

4 Your map is now oriented, and if you draw a line from your position on the map to a landmark (e.g. the top of a hill), you should find that this line points to the landmark in real life.

Compass types

Ancient Chinese

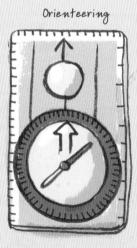

Orienteering

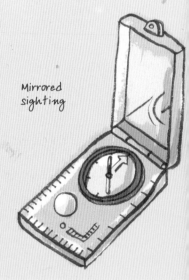

Mirrored sighting

Natural north

Because the Sun shines from the south, if you are in the northern hemisphere, you can tell which way is north by looking carefully at the trees. In the southern hemisphere, reverse all these signs, because the Sun shines from the north.

A dark rock will be lighter on the south-facing side.

DIY INSTANT COMPASS

 TRY THIS

The quickest way to make your own compass is to rub a needle with a piece of soft cloth. Rub it 30 times toward the needle point, always in the same direction. Now put the needle on a small leaf floating on water, or even just directly on the surface of the water, and it should line up so that the tip of the needle points north.

- Young trees will be lighter on the south side and darker on the north side.

- The branches on the south side of a tree will grow out sideways, but the branches on the north side will stick up.

- A tree on its own will usually have more moss on the north (shady side).

- Trees growing on a south-facing slope will be thicker and taller.

Lensatic

Button

Direct sighting

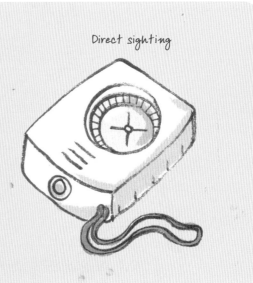

STAY THE COURSE

The bush plane dropped you off at the remote jungle airstrip, and after an hour of hard climbing you have reached the top of the nearest hill. You know your target—an extinct volcano that may be populated with animals unknown to science—lies somewhere in the clouds across the deep valley. But how will you get there? As soon as you plunge into the rainforest you will lose your way, and if you get lost in this jungle you may never come out. Your only hope is to use your map and your compass to maintain a bearing, which means picking a direction and sticking with it.

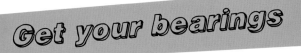

Get your bearings

Direction of travel arrow

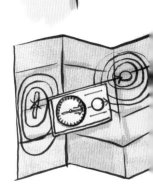

The first thing you need to do is take a bearing on the volcano. Get out your map and put your compass on it so that the edge of the compass draws a line from your position to the volcano. Turn the dial with the big arrow until it is pointing toward map north, and the little lines on the compass face are lined up with the north-south lines on the map. Now read the bearing off the dial—let's say it is 60°.

Now you need to get your bearing. Turn the dial until the 60° mark is lined up with the arrow showing which direction you are facing (the "direction of travel arrow"). Now hold the compass in front of you and turn around until the north pole of the compass (the tip of the red arrow) lines up with the big arrow. You should now be facing directly toward the volcano. Big deal—you already know where it is. But what about when you are down in the valley and you can't see the volcano? You will still know which way to go just by turning until the compass needle and the big arrow line up.

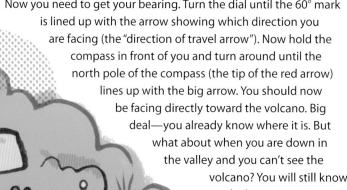

The long way round

Hacking your way through the jungle, you reach the edge of a swamp, filled with deadly quicksand and a very hungry alligator. Looks like you'll have to go round it, but won't this put you off course, so that the bearing you've been following is no good? Not if you know how to maintain a bearing, which means making adjustments for your detour. Use your compass to take four turns of 90° each: three to get round the swamp and the last one to get back on track. Count your paces between the first and second turn, and walk the same distance after the third turn. This will ensure that you get right back on course.

BIG BOTTOM GIRL

In 1850, the English scientist Francis Galton was exploring the southern African deserts when he saw a woman with an especially massive bottom. Galton was obsessed with measuring things, but he was too embarrassed to measure her butt with a ruler, so he used his sextant and his map drawing skills to work out the size of her bottom using mathematics.

When he wasn't measuring bottoms, Galton invented the weather map and a system for classifying fingerprints.

NAVIGATING BY THE STARS

Try not to get lost in the Antarctic mountains in winter: not only will it be cold enough to kill you in seconds with raging winds that knock you off your feet, but it will be hard to navigate back to base. The Sun never rises and your compass will go haywire because you are too near the southern magnetic pole. Your only hope is to use the stars—the same navigational tools that people have been using since earliest prehistoric times.

SEXTANT

You can use a sextant to measure the angle between a star (including our nearest star—the Sun) and the horizon. With this information you can calculate your latitude—your position north or south of the Equator. Navy navigators are still taught how to use the sextant in case their electronic systems get blown up in battle.

The sky at night

Look up on a cloudless night and you will see thousands of stars scattered across the sky. With just your eyes you can see around 2,000 stars at a time (if you have binoculars you can see around 50,000). These stars seem to move very slowly across the night sky, but in fact they are not moving—you are, or at least Earth is moving and taking you with it. As Earth rotates toward the east, the stars above seem to move from east to west, like the Sun and Moon. You can use this simple fact to work out north, south, east, and west.

Star movement at the North Pole

Star movement at the Equator

Star movement in between

Star tracking

Stars move very slowly so working out which way a star is moving just by looking at it is impossible. You need to watch the star against something close to hand. You can use two sticks stuck in the ground close together and upright, and track how a star moves between them. If you are in the northern hemisphere and the star moves left, it is to the north, if it moves right it is to the south, if it moves up the star is in the east, down and it is in the west.

Star shadow

Another method is to hang a string from a stick set in the ground at an angle. Lie on your back with the string by your eye and line it up with a star. Mark the point where the string touches the ground. Follow the star for ten minutes and then do it again. This is the same as the Sun stick method, with the string in place of the shadow (see page 131)—the first mark is in the west and the second is in the east.

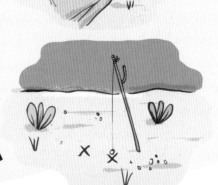

MORE NEXT PAGE

Finding north and south by the stars

The North or Pole Star, Polaris, is above the North Pole, so all the other stars seem to rotate around it. If you can find it you know which way is north. There is no bright star above the South Pole, but you can find south with the help of the constellation called the Southern Cross.

FIND THE NORTH STAR

- Find the Plow (also known as the Big Dipper or Ursa Major). The two stars in the outer edge of the "saucepan" point at the North Star, which is one of the brightest stars in the sky.

- Find Cassiopeia, a constellation that looks like a big "M" or "W." A line pointing straight through the inner angle of the "W" points to the North Star.

- The North Star is the last star in the "handle" of the "Little Dipper," also known as Ursa Minor.

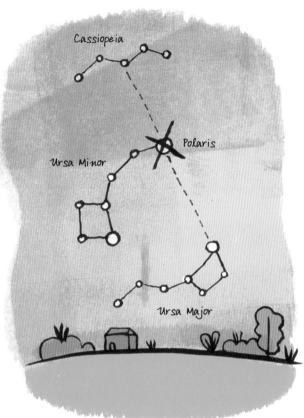

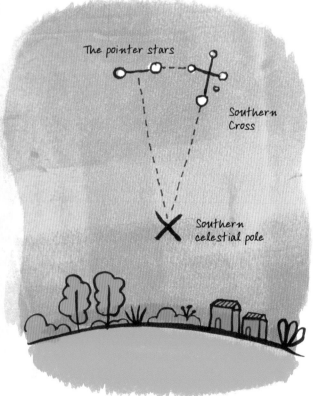

FIND THE SOUTHERN CELESTIAL POLE

- Find the Milky Way (a milky band across the sky).

- Follow it until you find a dark patch called the Coal Sack.

- Look for a cross of four stars, two of which are very bright. This is the Southern Cross.

- Near the Southern Cross are two bright stars— the pointer stars (Rigil Kent and Hadar). Draw an imaginary line between these stars. The point where this line intersects with a line extended from the long axis of the Southern Cross is the celestial south pole.

SASTRUGI SIGNS

If you are exploring in Antarctica, you don't want to get off course because the landscape is featureless so there are few landmarks to help you get back on track. A good tip is to use the sastrugi—wavy ridges in the snow, like sand dunes, formed by the wind, which run for great distances in parallel lines. Are you heading straight across them, along them, or at an angle to them? Memorize this information and use it to set your course.

By the horns of the Moon!

The Moon goes round Earth once every 28 days. We can only see it when the Sun shines on the side that is facing us. When the Sun shines on the whole of the facing side, we see a full Moon, and when it shines entirely on the opposite side, we can't see the Moon at all (this is called a "new Moon"). In between the Sun only lights up part of the Moon, so that we see a "crescent Moon."

You can use the crescent Moon as a quick way to find north or south, depending on your hemisphere. The tips of the crescent are known as the "horns." Imagine a straight line between the horns, extending down to the horizon. In the northern hemisphere this line points roughly south, and in the southern hemisphere it points roughly north.

EXPLORER BOOTCAMP

You are hiking across open country when you begin to notice worrying signs. The clouds of biting insects are getting frantic, and you have spotted several deer tearing at bushes in a frenzy. You stop to look at a spider's web; the spider is huddled up in one corner. Worst of all, the clouds seem to be moving against the wind. Looks like the weather is going to get bad— real bad. Luckily you packed your poncho and your boots are waterproof. Should you look for shelter under that tree, or beneath the overhanging bank of the empty river bed?

The midges are biting. Maybe a storm's coming. See page 151.

Does this spider know something we don't? See page 150.

EXPLORER'S ESSENTIALS

Packing for an explorer's adventure isn't like packing for the beach, although in both cases you should take a hat. Unless you are the Duke of Abruzzi, grandson of the king of Italy, who traveled to Alaska in 1897 with dozens of servants and porters, and four cast iron beds, you will probably have to plan carefully so that you can carry all the gear you need in a single backpack.

Boot up

Unless you are planning to fly or sail for the entire expedition, you will need to rely on your own two feet at some point, possibly making the right boots your most important piece of equipment. Your boots need to be a perfect mixture: light and flexible, but sturdy and waterproof, warm but not too sweaty. The exact boot will depend on where you are going.

BASIC HIKING BOOT

- For walking and exploring in forest, mountains, rough ground or grassland anywhere in the temperate zone (places that are not too hot and not too cold), this boot is best.

- It is tough but flexible and relatively lightweight, and will let your foot breathe.

JUNGLE BOOT

- Made from canvas and rubber to cope with wet ground and constant rainfall, waterproof below and quick-drying above.

- This boot is tough enough to resist thorns, insect bites, and snake fangs, but light enough not to overheat your feet.

MOUNTAIN BOOT

- Much more rigid than hiking boots, these boots are stiff and heavy but keep your feet warm and dry in snow and ice, and won't slip or buckle when jammed against a rock.

DESERT BOOT

- Usually made of suede, which keeps out hot sand but is very light and lets your feet breathe to stay relatively cool.

Bare necessities

Pack a few warm but light and quick-drying clothes, a sleeping bag suited to your destination (don't take a heavy, super-warm one to a jungle), waterproof jacket, fire-lighting equipment, first aid kit, maps, and compass, and a survival kit. This should be in a tough container like a tin, and should be kept on you at all times. It contains things like a button compass, fishing line and hook, lighter, wire saw, and a needle and thread.

Jacket

Backpack

First aid kit

Sleeping bag

Camping stove

Lighter

Compass

Map

Survival tin

Clothes

Fishing line and hook

Wire saw

DOUBLE UP

The best gear is stuff that is multi-use. For instance, when Norwegian polar explorer Fridtjof Nansen made the first crossing of Greenland in 1888, he used the groundsheet from his tent as both a sail for his sled and the bottom of a makeshift boat.

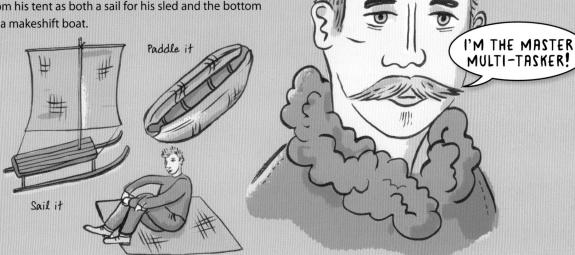

Paddle it

Sail it

Sit on it

I'M THE MASTER MULTI-TASKER!

THE RULE OF THREES

Explorers love stuff, like good boots or a nifty GPS tracker, but every good explorer knows that knowledge is way more important than stuff will ever be. The single most important thing an explorer should know is the "rule of threes." You could be naked on a desert island in a hurricane, and if you knew the rule of threes you would still be better off than someone equipped with everything from gloves that heat up to a pen that writes in outer space.

The magic number

The rule of threes goes like this:

- You can survive for three minutes without air

- You can survive for three hours without shelter

- You can survive for three days without water

- You can survive for three weeks without food

Why is this important? It tells you everything you need to know about your priorities in a survival situation. Priorities are things you should do first. Explorers often find themselves in dangerous situations, and if they want to survive, they need to get their priorities straight. The rule of threes tells you what to do and in what order.

② As you struggle to get out from under a pile of stuff, the water closes over your head. You are now underwater. It will take you a minute and a half to get free, and two minutes to get out of the cabin into the open water. Should you try to grab your survival bag first, or get out now?

⑤ Should you look about for a stream of freshwater so you can wash out your mouth, or get to work right away making a shelter from the wind, even though you are desperately thirsty?

Three at sea

1 Imagine you are sailing solo across the ocean when a strong wind blows up out of nowhere. Your boat hits a submerged reef, and water floods into the cabin.

3 The rule of threes tells you that you can't afford the time you need to grab your survival bag. Get out now or drown!

4 You thrash clear of the overturned boat and are washed up on to the beach of a desert island, choking and spitting from all the seawater you've swallowed.

EEERGH!

6 You can survive for three days without water, but if you stay out in the storm without shelter you'll be dead in three hours. Build that shelter!

7 Next morning you crawl out of your shelter and find a box of cookies that's washed ashore from your boat. You're starving, but should you scarf them, or start looking for water?

TIME FOR A BATH?

8 Find water first—you can make it for three weeks without eating. Also, digesting food soaks up water from your body, so leave the biscuits until later.

9 Two weeks later you are rescued— hungry and thin, but still alive thanks to the rule of threes.

FIRE STARTER

A fire can help to keep you warm, provide light at night-time, boil water to purify it and cook food to make it safe and tasty. But what if you are swept over a waterfall and lose all your equipment, including your lighter and matches? Would you be able to start a fire to dry your clothes and get warm?

The right stuff

Tinder

Kindling

Fuel

It takes more than just wood to build a fire. In fact you need three different kinds of stuff: tinder, kindling, and fuel. Tinder is very light stuff that will catch alight from a single spark. Kindling consists of small twigs—no thicker than your little finger—that will get your fire going. Fuel ranging from sticks to big logs is the stuff that keeps the fire going.

> Think ahead—it's no good collecting dry tinder and kindling only for them to get wet. Prepare somewhere dry and rain-proof to store them.

How to start a fire by rubbing two bits of wood together

Starting a fire using only stuff from nature is the big challenge. Somehow you need to get enough heat to create a spark and/or get tinder smouldering. You do this by rubbing together two bits of wood, but you have to know how to rub them together. The simplest method is called a fire plow. Grab a grown-up and try it out in your back yard.

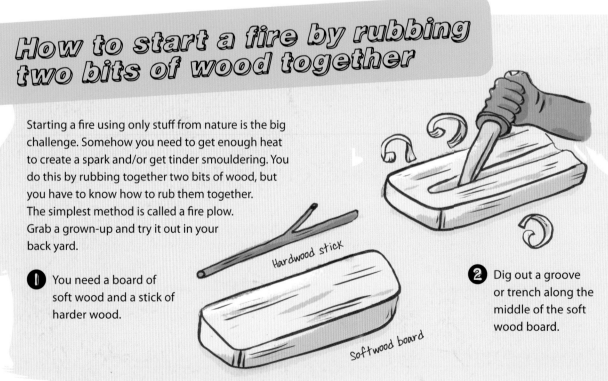

Hardwood stick

Softwood board

1 You need a board of soft wood and a stick of harder wood.

2 Dig out a groove or trench along the middle of the soft wood board.

Fire starting cheats

1 Flint and steel. Strike the flint (actually a metal alloy called ferrocium) with a steel blade and you'll be rewarded with a shower of sparks. Use the sparks to ignite your tinder.

2 A magnifying glass will focus the rays of the Sun to a hot spot.

3 You can use a fist-sized ball of polished ice as a magnifying glass.

4 Polish the bottom of a soda can with chocolate or toothpaste and you will get a very shiny mirror that reflects sunlight onto a single point—but you will have to polish for hours!

5 Touch some steel wool to the end of a battery.

3 Rub the stick backward and forward along the groove.

4 If you do it hard enough and fast enough, wood dust will collect at the end of the groove, and your rubbing will heat the dust until it starts smoking.

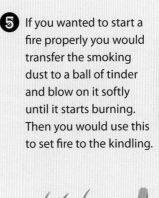

5 If you wanted to start a fire properly you would transfer the smoking dust to a ball of tinder and blow on it softly until it starts burning. Then you would use this to set fire to the kindling.

CAMPING OUT

After a hard day's exploring in the Mountains of the Moon, the Home of the Giants or the Land of Fire (all real places!), you need somewhere safe, warm, and comfortable to relax, cook a nice meal and get a good night's sleep. Choose your campsite wisely, however, or you could get woken up by falling branches, rivers of flooding water, rampaging wild animals, or possibly all of the above.

The ideal campsite

Think about where the Sun will be through the day. Do you want shade or sunshine?

Trees make a good windbreak.

Don't build a fire too close to your tent.

Lovely fresh water.

The best campsite will be on flat ground protected from the wind and close to fresh water but far enough away from flood danger. It will be near trees, which block the wind and provide fuel for fires, but not underneath them. There will be a good spot to build your fire. Dig a trench or drainage ditch around your tent so that if it rains, the water flows around and away from you, instead of into your sleeping bag.

Camp at established campsites when possible, and remember that good campsites are found, not made.

Where not to camp

At the bottom of a valley. This is likely to be wet and marshy, with a risk of flooding. Also, cold air sinks at night, so valley floors can get cold.

Under a tree. Even healthy-looking branches may fall on you in a strong wind.

At the foot of a cliff. Rocks may fall on you, and water will flow down into your tent.

At the bottom of a snowy slope. You could get hit by an avalanche.

At the foot of a cliff. Rocks may fall on you, and water will flow down into your tent.

Across an animal track. You might get woken by a wild visitor.

In a gully or dry river-bed. If it rains, there could be a flash-flood.

TRY THIS AT HOME

TRAILBLAZING

Trailblazing means marking out a trail using signs that other explorers can follow. In the wild it is a good way for explorers to help each other out. After all, if you learned the hard way to avoid that bear-infested cave, why not warn others? There are different signs you can use; here are some from the international language of trailblazing, which you can mark on rocks with chalk, carve into trees or spell out with stones.

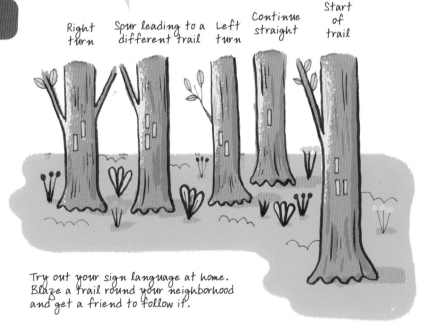

Right turn

Spur leading to a different trail

Left turn

Continue straight

Start of trail

Try out your sign language at home. Blaze a trail round your neighborhood and get a friend to follow it.

WEATHER WISE

Successful explorers know when to travel and when to take shelter, because you don't want to be caught out in the open during a storm. At best you and your equipment will get wet; at worst you could die from the cold, get swept away by flood waters, be hit by lightning or falling trees, or get blasted by a hurricane or tornado force winds.

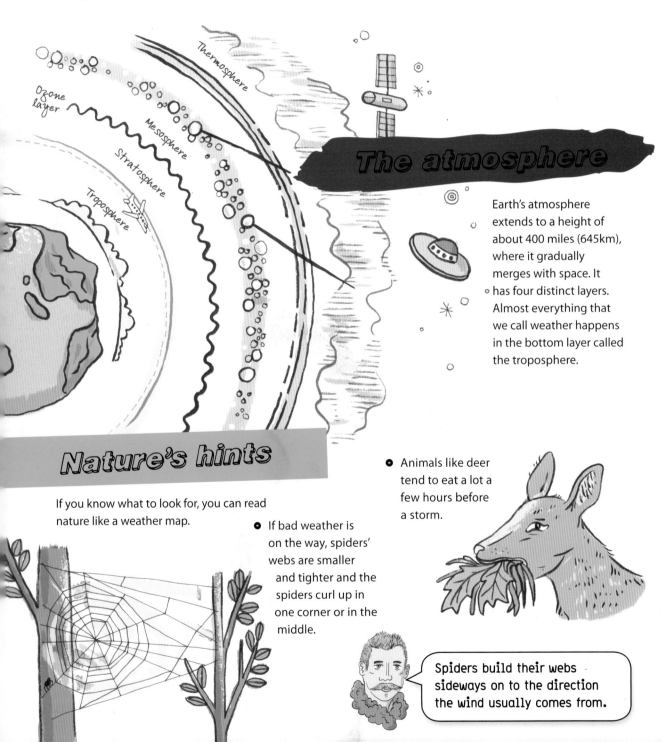

The atmosphere

Earth's atmosphere extends to a height of about 400 miles (645km), where it gradually merges with space. It has four distinct layers. Almost everything that we call weather happens in the bottom layer called the troposphere.

Nature's hints

If you know what to look for, you can read nature like a weather map.

- If bad weather is on the way, spiders' webs are smaller and tighter and the spiders curl up in one corner or in the middle.

- Animals like deer tend to eat a lot a few hours before a storm.

Spiders build their webs sideways on to the direction the wind usually comes from.

Written in the sky

A key to predicting the weather is to watch the clouds. Clouds can be very high, close to the ground or in-between.

- Fluffy low clouds in a blue sky usually mean good weather.

- Sky-covering clouds, whether low, medium, or high, often mean rain.

- Layers of cloud one on top of the other, or a huge fluffy cloud that goes up high into the sky both mean storms.

- A cloud that goes up and spreads out at the top can mean lightning is on the way.

DIY WEATHER STICK

TRY THIS

Cut a straight stick from a willow, birch or fir tree—it should be about 16 inches (40cm) long and about1 inch (3cm) wide at the cut end. Nail it to the outside of a tree house or garden shed, so that it sticks straight out sideways. If it twists down, bad weather is on the way; up and good weather is due. This trick was used by Native Americans in the US northeast and eastern Canada to predict the weather.

Down—get ready to be wet

Up—sunshine is coming your way

- If the smoke from your campfire goes straight up, expect good weather.

- If airplane trails in the sky hang around for two hours, bad weather is on the way.

- Biting insects like midges and mosquitoes become more active an hour or so before a storm is due to hit.

STORM WARNING

Hiking across the mountains, you see the flicker of lightning in the distance and feel the first drops of rain on the wind. An electrical storm is coming! On the lonely mountainside you are in real danger of being blasted to a crisp. What should you do?

Danger! High voltage

Lightning is an incredibly strong blast of electricity that wants to get from the clouds into the ground, and which travels through anything that sticks up from the ground. That includes you, so you need to find somewhere safe.

SHOCK HORROR!

PLACES TO SHELTER

- Inside. Get into a car or building. Close the doors and windows and try not to touch anything metal.

- A grove of low trees. If trees or bushes are thick and low, and away from tall trees, they can make a good shelter.

- A deep cave. But stay away from the entrance.

AVOID

- Trees. Tall trees are likely to attract lightning.

- Open-sided shelters. This includes everything from bus shelters to umbrellas.

- High ground. If you are on a hill or mountain, try to get off it!

- Holes. If lightning strikes flat ground, the electricity may travel toward a hole or dip.

Lightning proof yourself

Make yourself less attractive to lightning by...

1 Crouching down on the ground and curling up into the smallest ball possible, with your hands round the back of your neck. Only the balls of your feet should be on the ground. This is called the lightning crouch.

2 Get rid of anything metal, including ice axes, watches, and backpacks with metal frames.

3 Sit on a coiled up rope or a piece of wood and roll into a fetal position. Don't let anything touch the ground.

HAIR-RAISING

Sometimes before lightning hits a person they will become charged with static electricity. If your hair starts to stand on end and your skin tingles, look out! Get to a safe place immediately or if there isn't one right next to you, get into the lightning crouch.

Tornado trouble

A tornado is a spiral of air that sucks things up from the ground. Winds can move at hundreds of miles an hour in a tornado, and sticks, rocks, and other deadly things get blasted around like bullets. If you are caught in a tornado, shelter in a ditch or hole and kneel down with your hands over your head.

A

acute mountain sickness (AMS) 79

adaptations 33

aerial circumnavigation 115

aerodynamics 120

airplane crashes 18-19, 114, 115, 124, 125

airplane trails 151

Africa 9, 11, 16, 25, 26, 28-29

airships 117, 124

aircraft 116-117

Amazon rainforest 8, 13, 17, 19

Amazon River 88, 105, 111

Amundsen, Roald 56, 60, 61, 117, 124, 125

ancient civilizations 8, 32

Andes Mountains 84

Andrée, Salomon 60

Angel, Jimmy 115

Angel Falls 115

Antarctica 35, 48, 61, 81, 139

appendectomy 47

Arctic Ocean 124

Arctic region 52, 124

Asia 35

Atacama Desert 34

atmospheric layers 150

Australia 43, 65

avalanches 76-77, 149

aviation 18-19, 114-125

B

balloons 60, 117

bathyscape 91

bear attacks 58, 67

bears 52, 58, 67

bees 15, 37

belay and self-belay techniques 72-73, 74

berries 68-69

big cats 9, 27, 28, 29

bird strikes 121

birds 93, 121

black bears 67

black snake 25

Bleriot, Louis 117

boots 142

botflies 15, 19

Bouvet Island 89

brown bears 67

brown snake 25

bull sharks 105

Burton, Richard 28-29

bush plane 116

bushmaster 25

Byrd, Richard 124, 125

C

cactus 38

Cambyses' army 32

camel taming 43

camels 30, 33, 42-43

campsites 148-149

candiru 105

canoes and kayaks 91, 104, 106, 108-109

Cape buffalo 9, 27

capsized boats 109

caravel 91

caterpillars 15

celestial navigation 93, 136, 137

Challenger Deep 91

Charcot, Jean-Baptiste 95

cliffs 37, 149

clouds 93, 151

clues from nature 36-37, 68, 93, 133, 150-152

coconuts 98

collier 91

Columbus, Christopher 100

compass bearings 134-135

compasses 97, 130, 132-133, 134-135

Congo 16

constellations 93, 136-138, 139

contour lines 129
coral reefs 119
cork hat 44
Corps of Discovery 107
Courthauld, Augustine 55
crevasses 78
crocodiles 12
Crusoe, Robinson 98, 99
currach 91

D

de Orellana, Francisco 111
Death Zone 78
Deepsea Challenger 91, 102
desert boot 142
deserts 32-47
detours 135
dirigible 117
diving bell 91, 102
diving suit 102
dog-sleds 56-7
dogs 56
double fisherman's knot 75
dry bag 111
Duke of Abruzzi 55, 142

E

Earhart, Amelia 114, 119
Egypt 32
El Dorado 17, 111
electric eels 105
elephant attacks 23
elephant riding 22
elephants 22-23
Ellsworth, Lincoln 124
emergency "grab bag" 96

emergency landing technique
    122-123
Endeavour 91
Endurance 61
equipment 72, 80, 81, 83,
    90, 96, 110, 111, 121,
    132-133, 134, 135, 142-143
explorers 8, 16, 28-29, 51,
    55, 56, 60-61, 65, 77, 82,
    83, 84-85, 91, 95, 100-101,
    107, 111, 114, 124-125, 135,
    143

F

Fawcett, Colonel Percy 17
Fay, Mike 23
fer-de-lance 25
figure of eight loop 75
fins 102
fire starting techniques
    146-147
first aid 14, 15, 19, 24, 41,
    47, 59
fish 13, 69, 89, 105
fish trap 69
floatation aid 13
folklore 65, 71
food and drink sources 22,
    25, 53, 56, 66-67, 70, 98,
    97, 144
food safety 67, 68-67, 97
forests 64-68

Fossett, Steve 115
fossils 65
Franklin, Sir John 51
freediving 103
Freuchen, Peter 59
frogs 37
frostnip 59
frostbite 59, 82
fuel sources 39, 146

G

Galton, Francis 135
Gardner Island 119
glaciers 78
globe luxation 47

Gobi Desert 35
Gremlin Special 18
group safety 46, 74, 103

H

Habeler, Peter 79
Harry the camel 43
headwear and hats 11, 44-45
heatstroke 41
helicopters 117, 118
Hempleman-Adams, David 82
Heyerdahl, Thor 91, 101

hiking boot 142
hippos 9, 26
Horrocks, John Ainsworth 43
Hosking, Craig 118
Hubbard, Mina 111
Hunt, John 77, 83
huskies 56
hydration 39, 97

I

ice axe 72
ice hazards 120
igloo 54
Inca 8
indigenous people 9, 11, 18, 25, 29, 39, 44, 52-53, 70-71, 92-93
Indonesia 9
insects 15, 19, 33, 37, 41, 69, 111, 151
Inuit people 52-53, 56
Iron Boat 107
Irvine, Sandy 65, 82
islands 89, 92, 98-99
Italia 125

J

Jolliet, Louis 110
Josephine Ford 125
jungle boot 11, 142
jungles 8-25
junks 91, 101

K

kangaroo rats 33
Karman line 115
kepi hat 45
ketch 91
Kilauea Volcano 118
king cobra 25
knots 75
Knox-Johnston, Robin 91
Koepcke, Juliane 19
Kon-Tiki 91, 101, 107

L

landing aircraft 118-119
latitude and longitude 129, 136
leadership and planning 60, 61, 83
leeches 14
leopards 27
Lewis and Clark 107
life raft 90
lift 120
lightning 152-153
lightning crouch 153
Lindbergh, Charles 116
lions 9, 27, 28
Livingstone, Dr. David 16
lizards 30

Lukla Airport 119

M
....

machetes 10, 15

Mallory, George 65, 82

map folding 128-129

map reading 129

Marquette, Father Jacques 110

Masai tribe 25

Mbuti pygmies 11

Mekong giant catfish 89

message in a bottle 99

Messner, Reinhold 79

meteorites 48

Micronesians 92

Middle East 35

migration 48

mirage 41

Mississippi River 110

Moon horns 139

mortar 77

mosquitoes 37, 111, 151

moss 133

Mount Erebus 81

Mount Everest 64, 65, 71, 79, 82-83, 119

mountain boot 142

mountain climbing 72-74

mountains 50, 70-85, 115, 152

mushrooms 68

N
....

Nansen, Fridtjof 143

"natural" north 133

navigation 92, 93, 121, 126-39

Nepal 70, 119

New Guinea 18

Nile River 9, 16, 28, 88

Nobile, Umberto 117, 124, 125

Noonan, Fred 114, 119

Norge 117, 124, 125

North America 51, 110

North (Pole) Star 138

Northwest Passage 51

Nuestra Senora de Atocha 103

O
....

oceans 88-103

orienteering 132-135

orienteering compass 132

oxygen supply 77, 79, 82, 83, 144, 145

P
....

Patterson, Colonel John Henry 29

Peary, Robert 124

penguins 48

Peruvian Alps 85

piranhas 13

Pizarro, Francisco 8

plants and trees 10, 15, 38, 68-69, 133, 149, 151, 152

poisonous and venomous animals and plants 15, 24, 25, 38, 41, 98

polar bears 52, 58, 67

polar regions 50-61

Polaris 138

Poles, North and South 50, 56, 60, 115, 124-125, 130, 138

Polynesia 92

Polynesians 92-93

Poon Lim 97

portage 108

protective clothing 11, 40, 41, 44-45, 53, 80, 81, 83, 111, 142-3

prusik knot 75

purification (water) 37

Q
....

quicksand 20-21

R
....

rafts 13, 91, 107

Raleigh, Sir Walter 17

Ralston, Aron 46

rappelling 80-81

rattle snake 25

river beds 149

rivers 88, 104-111

Robinson Crusoe Island 99

rock art 33

Rogozov, Leonid 47

Rub al Khali 35

Rule of Threes 144-145

S

safari hat 45

Sahara Desert 33, 39

sailing 94, 95

sand dunes 34, 45

sandstorms 40

sastrugi ridges 139

savanna 26-27

scorpions 41

Scott, Robert Falcon 56, 60

screw roll technique 109

scuba diving 102

seamarks and landmarks 93

seals 48

seaplane 116

seasickness 94

Selkirk, Alexander 99

sextant 135, 136

Shackleton, Ernest 60, 61, 81

sharks 94, 95, 105

shelter 54-55, 144, 152-153

Sherpas 70-71

ships and boats 90-91, 143

shipwrecks 89, 103

signs and signals 85, 99, 149

Simpson, Joe 85

smoke 151

snake bites 24

snakes 9, 24, 25

snorkeling 102

snow goggles 53

snowshoes 53

solar still 39

South Africa 89

South America 9, 16, 17, 34, 89, 111, 115

Southern Cross 138

Speke, John Hanning 28-29

spider webs 150

S.S. Republic 103

Stanley, Henry Morton 16

star shadow technique 137

star tracking technique 137

static electricity 153

stick charts 92

stinging trees 15

storms 95, 121, 152-153

stove location 55

submarines 91, 102

subterranean water 36

Suhaili 91

Sun stick technique 131, 137

sunstroke 41

surgery 47

survival strategies 19, 39, 77, 78, 82, 97, 98-99, 144-145

swimming safety 13, 94, 105

T

tagelmust 44

taiga 64

taipan 25

tepui 115

Tibet 70

ticks 15

tiger snake 25

Titanic 103

Toby the pig 95

tok tokkie beetle 33

tooth extraction 47

tornadoes 153

tracheotomy 47

trailblazing 149

Transantarctic Mountains 50

transoceanic rowboat 90

transpiration 38

treasure hunting 89, 103

Trieste 91

Tristan de Cunha 89

"true" north and south 130-131

Tuareg tribe 39, 44

U
....

underwater exploration
102-103

United States 65, 110, 107

urine 39, 44, 77

V
....

valleys 149

vegetation layers 10

Viking longship 91

volcanoes 80-81, 118

W
....

watches 131

water, locating 36-37,
38-39, 97

water pressure 102, 103

wayfinding skills 93

weather and climate 76,
93, 95, 120-121, 150-153

weather stick 151

Western Desert 32

whirlpools 104

wildlife encounters 12, 13,
14, 15, 19, 22-23, 24,
26-27, 58, 66-67, 94

Wollemi Pines 65

wolves 66

wound sutures 47

Y
....

yacht 90

yaks 70

Yates, Simon 85

Yeti 65

Z
....

Z, Lost City of 17

Zheng He, Admiral 91, 101

1st Edition
Published September 2012

Conceived by Weldon Owen in partnership with Lonely Planet
Produced by Weldon Owen Ltd

Northburgh House, 10 Northburgh Street, London, EC1V 0AT, UK

weldonowenpublishing.com

Copyright © 2012 Weldon Owen Publishing

WELDON OWEN LTD
Managing Director Sarah Odedina
Publisher Corinne Roberts
Creative Director Sue Burk
Sales Director Laurence Richard
Sales Manager, North America Ellen Towell
Designer Vivien Sung
Illustrator James Gulliver Hancock/The Jacky Winter Group
Editor Lachlan McLaine
Production Director Dominic Saraceno
Prepress Controller Tristan Hanks
Index Puddingburn Publishing Services

10 9 8 7 6 5 4 3 2 1

Published by
Lonely Planet Publications Pty Ltd ABN 36 005 607 983
90 Maribyrnong St, Footscray, Victoria 3011, Australia

ISBN 978 -1-7432-1425-1

Printed and bound in China by 1010 Printing Int Ltd

A WELDON OWEN PRODUCTION

Disclaimer
Weldon Owen and Lonely Planet take pride in doing our best to get the facts right in putting together the information in this book, but occasionally something slips past our beady eyes. Therefore we make no warranties about the accuracy or completeness of the information in the book and to the maximum extent permitted, we disclaim all liability. Wherever possible, we will endeavour to correct any errors of fact at reprint.

Kids—if you want to try any of the activities in this book, please ask your parents first! Parents—all outdoor activities carry some degree of risk, and we recommend that anyone participating in these activities be aware of the risks involved and seek professional instruction and guidance. None of the health/medical information in this book is intended as a substitute for professional medical advice; always seek the advice of a qualified practitioner.

The author would like to thank Lachlan McLaine, and to dedicate the book to two little explorers, Finn and Isaac.

Also available in the series

Country series books

City series books

LONELY PLANET OFFICES

Australia Head Office
Locked Bag 1, Footscray, Victoria 3011
phone 03 8379 8000
fax 03 8379 8111

USA
150 Linden St, Oakland, CA 94607
phone 510 250 6400
toll free 800 275 8555
fax 510 893 8572

UK
Media Centre, 201 Wood Lane,
London W12 7TQ
phone 020 8433 1333
fax 020 8702 0112